MAGDA PARASIDIS

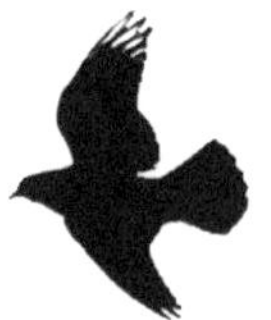

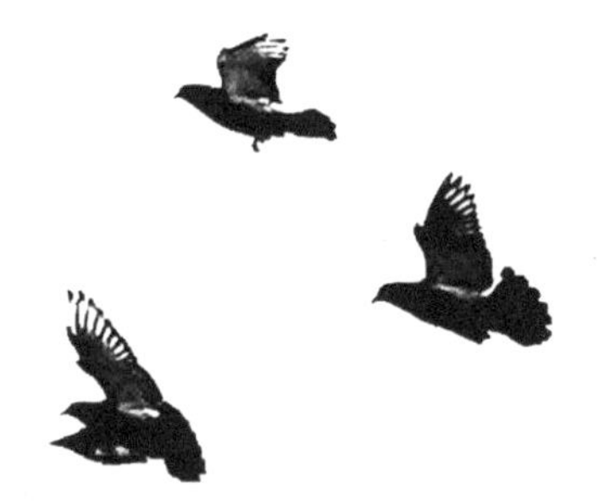

one/two

Also by Magda Parasidis
Ghosts in Sunlight

one/two

MAGDA PARASIDIS

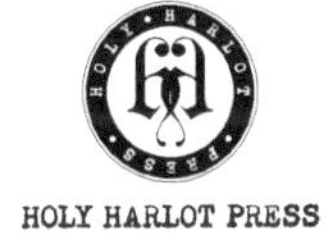

HOLY HARLOT PRESS

holyharlotpress@gmail.com

One/Two
Magda Parasidis
First Edition
ISBN: 979-8-9925646-0-0

Released by Holy Harlot Press 2026
Columbus / New York / Athens

Holy Harlot Press is an independent book publisher dedicated to supporting the work of artists and thinkers. We are devoted to the idea that reading, thinking and study are everyday revolutionary practices. Through books, art, and care, we incubate autonomous visions of life, free from the constraints of capital, in service to the commune.

Design: Sierra Lawhead
Creative Director: Magda Parasidis
Cover Photos: Magda Parasidis

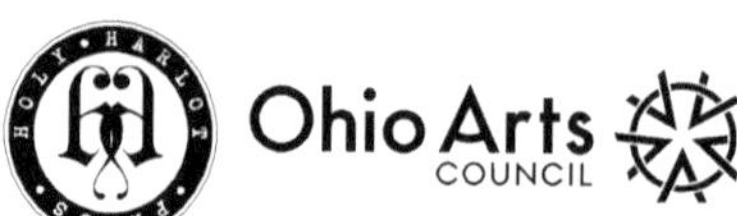

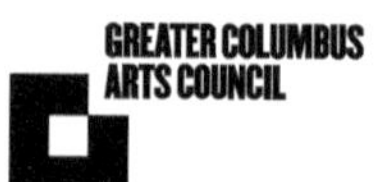

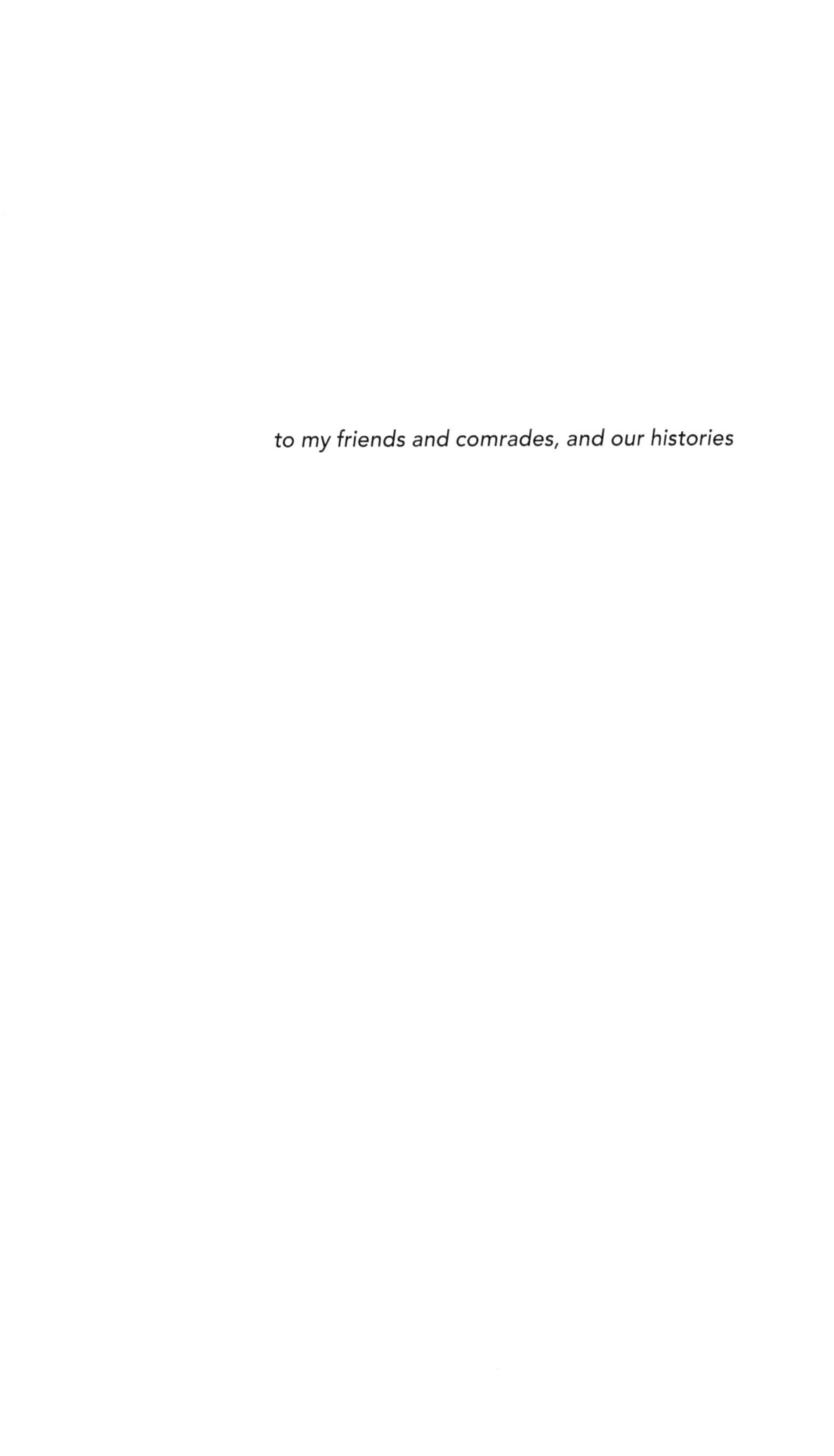

to my friends and comrades, and our histories

CONTENTS

One / 1

Diptychs / 15

Two / 57

Diptychs / 73

Photo Index / 127

Notes / 131

Afterword / 137

Acknowledgments / 147

Photography and film taught me how to make sense of this situation: that a person or place could be both incontestably present and always already passed. That the world which we inhabit is always being shadowed by other worlds whose persistence demands something of us. Now, I want to understand how these lessons are essential to a certain experience of migration – in other words, how it is lived by those who made the journey and those who grew up in its wake.

/ George Kouvaros

...[she] knows the parameters of the real – [she] sees what is included and what is left out and [she] is now able to set sail for another place, a place that is neither the home [she] left, nor the home to which [she] wants to return.

/ Jack Halberstam

one/

BIRDSONG/

After losing a country,
a language,
my new anthem is in the sound of the street.

The fugitive's birdsong:
city flocks taking flight,
beats tumbling out windows.

I WANT TO MAKE SOMETHING OF EVERY PHOTOGRAPH /

I collage my lost world
and gather pictures as little ghosts of my heat.
The long-past narratives are urgent again.
I inhabit histories in the present
and the children need a witness.

THE PLACES INSIDE /

Me and all my ghettos -
Athens / Cairo / Alexandria / Queens
Petroupoli / Subra / Astoria / Bournazi

The ghettos you don't want to know about
The loaded word
The histories, your history
/and the others you acquired.

Migrations, displacements, expulsions.
Cellular history, genetic memory

Our many hoods coalesced
And made something of us.

THE MAGDALENE /

A confession of faith
    in the man from the eastern ghetto.
    All my good comes out of the same Nazareth.
He called her by her name
    the name of ancient lands long gone
    that sit still on the shore of Galilee.
More cartographer than renegade
    She looks to her own maps
    and to those emissaries of the cool
    spirit-moved in the direction of their flow.

How to reconnect to her namesake,
    that most beloved of disciples?
What with addiction, anger, angst
    her own 7 demons in *city flesh*
    and the loneliness that has nothing of solitude's pleasures.

The years
    the near-death, the passage, the recovering, the re-descent,
    the refinement.
Woman-fatigue belief
    that something soon-come.
Like that time so close to the shadow.
    White blaze under closed eyelids in the dark,
    kindled by the radiance of mercy.
    Light-producing in the midst of death-breaths.
I could not be further from mystic,
what with my hell-bent powder diet.
But the prayer is desperate. constant. clear.
A steady burn. oil lamp lit.
Still alive at dawn.

There's no roadside memorial in my name.
I don't live or die on that block.
A dilettante ever-stranger on a stranger's site,
    where we have trouble
    naming histories and native truths.
I go back, and back, and back again
    to reckon with my own origin.

Oh, and I romanticize, surely I do.
    Those otherworld figures I encounter
    in repose on village stoops, on rickshawed terraces,
    in all their sun-creviced beauty.
Who are these figures with so much embodied resolve?
    Fierce queens, languidly focused kings.
    Saturated power-presence against the mountainside.
They are of a different place, an ancestral place:
    A chasm between where I stayed and where I'm from.
    And yet, the people from both wear poverty as second skin.
And I, devoted to dermal study.

NOSTOS /

If I do feel nostos
it's for a time/place imagined
remembrance of a mirage-self,
something to do with girlhood health & vitality.

This child I haven't been.
A child of where earth meets sea,
of sun-ripened peaches and dripping watermelons,
bleached hair at her crown and winter skin sand-smoothed.

This wonder-self
is the what if of migration,
the what if I didn't know dislocation.
Seeing my sallowness,
my sullenness, dullness, roughness -
    symptoms of this other *project projected.*
A sense that home might be elsewhere,
freedom in a place already lost.

A LOVE LANGUAGE /

my favorite fruit are those eaten whole
figs plums grapes nectarines apricots
berries of all sorts
no skin to peel

THE CEILING /

Hands empty of trinkets and playthings
I rely on visions, not possessions
to keep my wonder intact
and to make space between myself and the girlhood tedium.

A color, enough to ignite a dreamscape.
Transparent fuchsia, metallic pink,
and chrome purple wrappers at the corner store.
Cotton candy blue melting on luna park lips.
Yellow 25 cent lemonheads sucked on the benches.
The supermarket gallon of radiator-melted ice cream soup
white, brown and pink in a swirl,
a first lesson in abstraction.

Or the lacquered red coming down the block
to pick up the courtyard's bombshell
vibrating subwoofers in the trunk,
making beige leather look like a hallucination.
Pulling up to iridescent puddle rainbows of pooled motor oil,
and me, wondering,
Is this the map of what might be?

Fresh from sleep,
already starting in on day-dreaming.
I leave this world for a while, for the one on the ceiling.
It's the white, the stark white popcorn ceiling,
and the Sunday morning sunrays catching the floating dust
that are my soothsayers and my church.

Solace as my eyes connect the plaster dots,
waiting, unrushed, for the images to appear.
The most unlikely images,

the perfectly executed drawings I could never manage by hand.
Extraordinary revelations, shapeshifting above me,
and then, the playful risk
to leave the just fully-formed image
let your eyes scan far away at a distance,
daring yourself to go back and find it again.
And you do find it, and it gives you a jolt of joy.
Little girl thrill of making something out of nothing.
Thrift, even in my earliest flights.

Here, now, I'm in those blessed recesses of memory
that feel outside of time / *time held*
past and present at once
with the frequency of the divine belonging to childhood.
The body is reminded of having been,
its sensations lived, felt, archived.

Ordinariness opening up spaces inside us to intuit
the simple / the good.
Unnameable now
as there are no words here, just comfort.
I'm weightless, content, resting.
Pleasure is easy to locate here
in the dust made visible,
in the soft recesses of the pillow,
on the ceiling come alive.
slow. soft. warm
a non-place
a preface.

BLUE /

The color blue
blue/white
blue/black

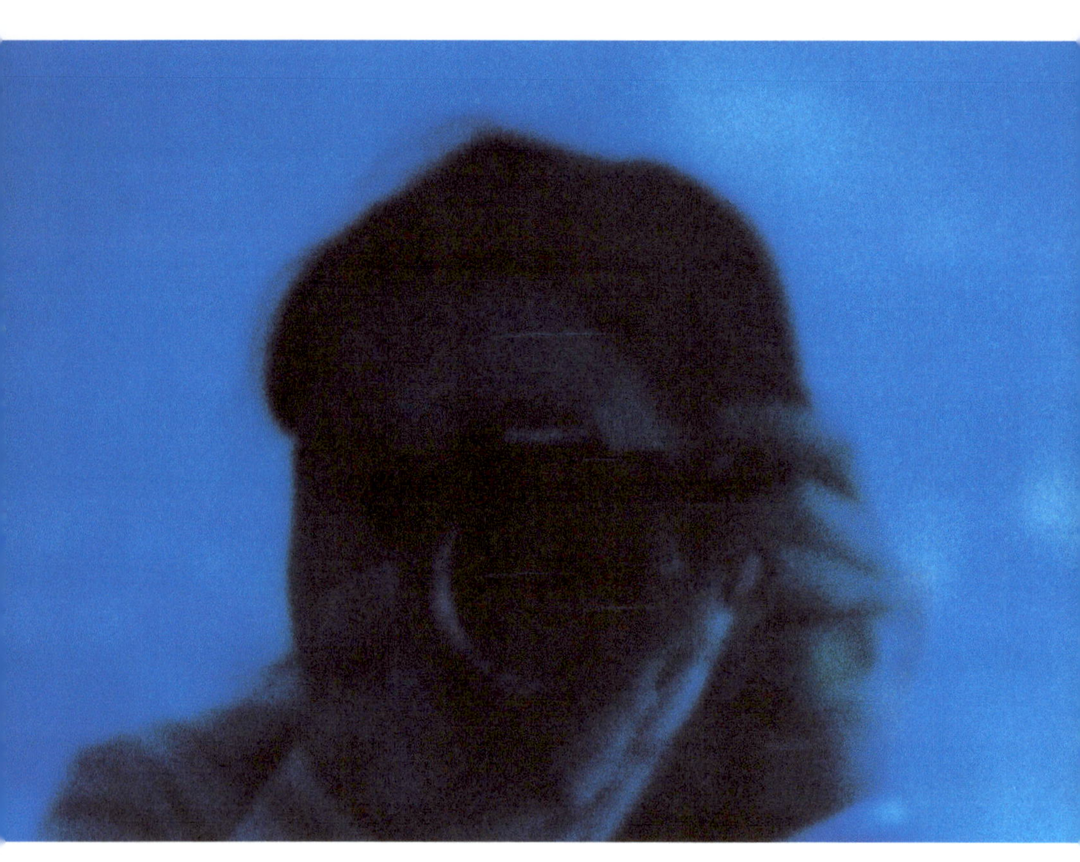

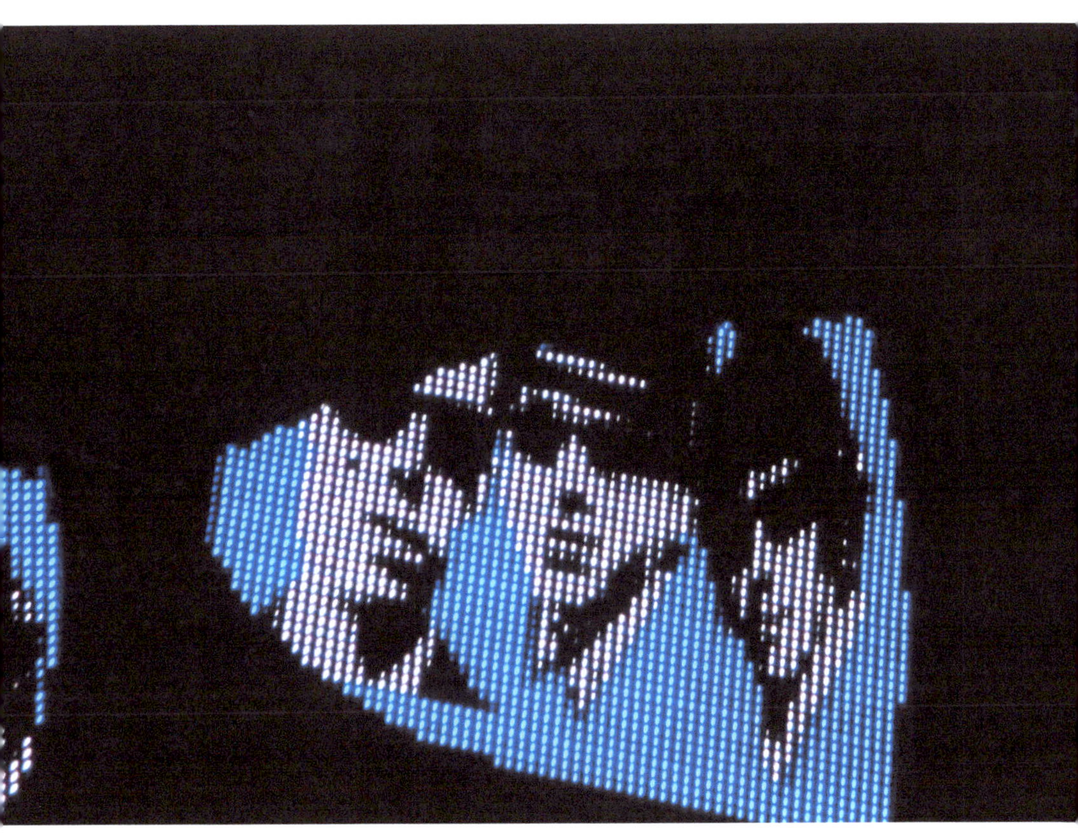

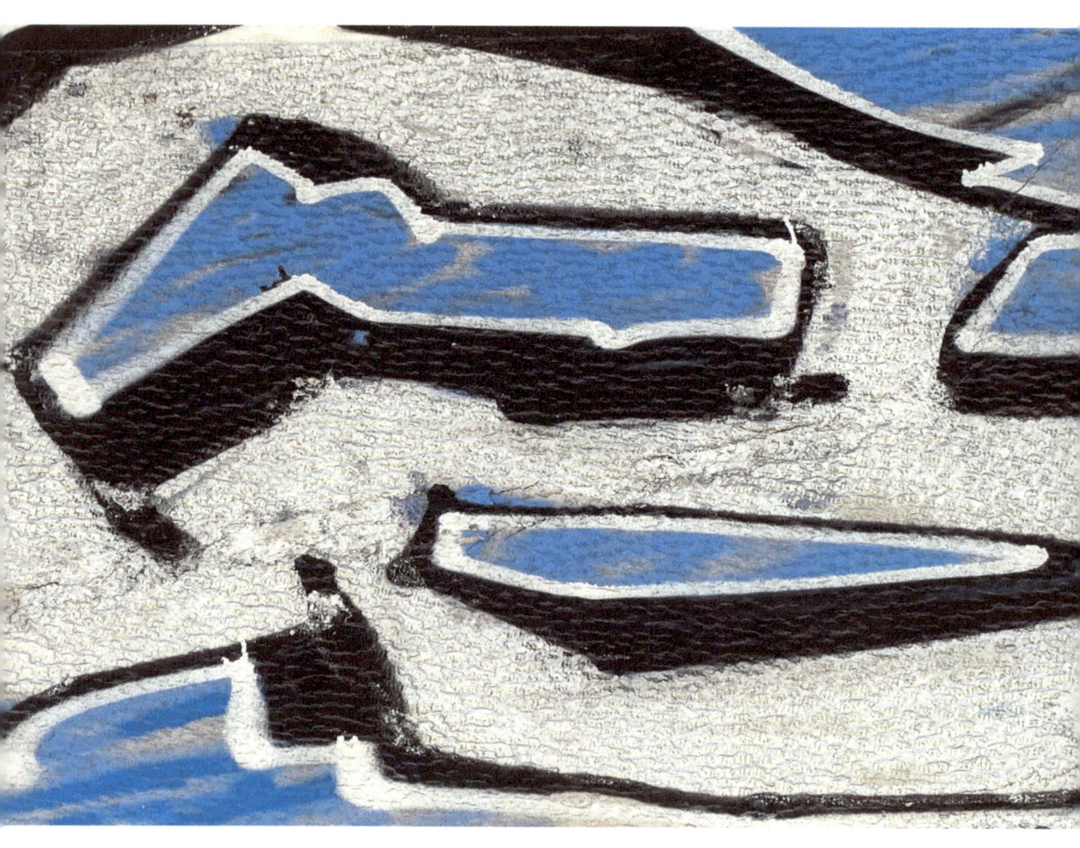

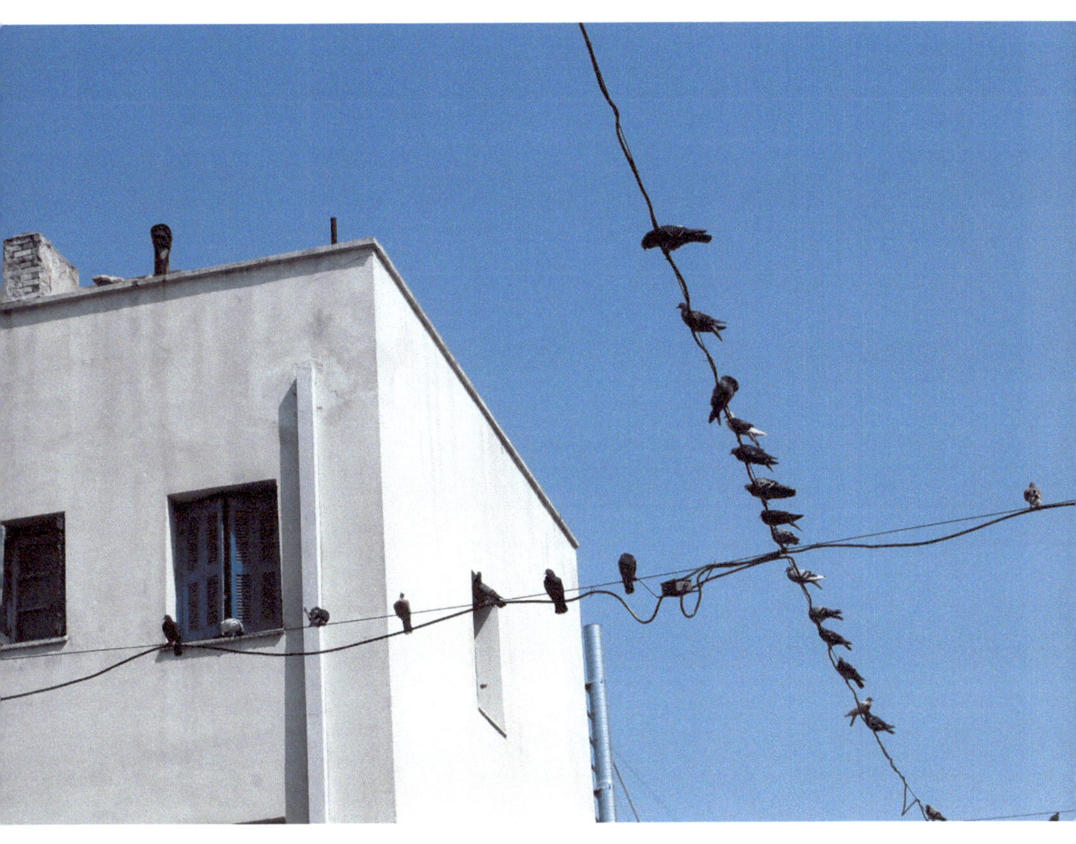

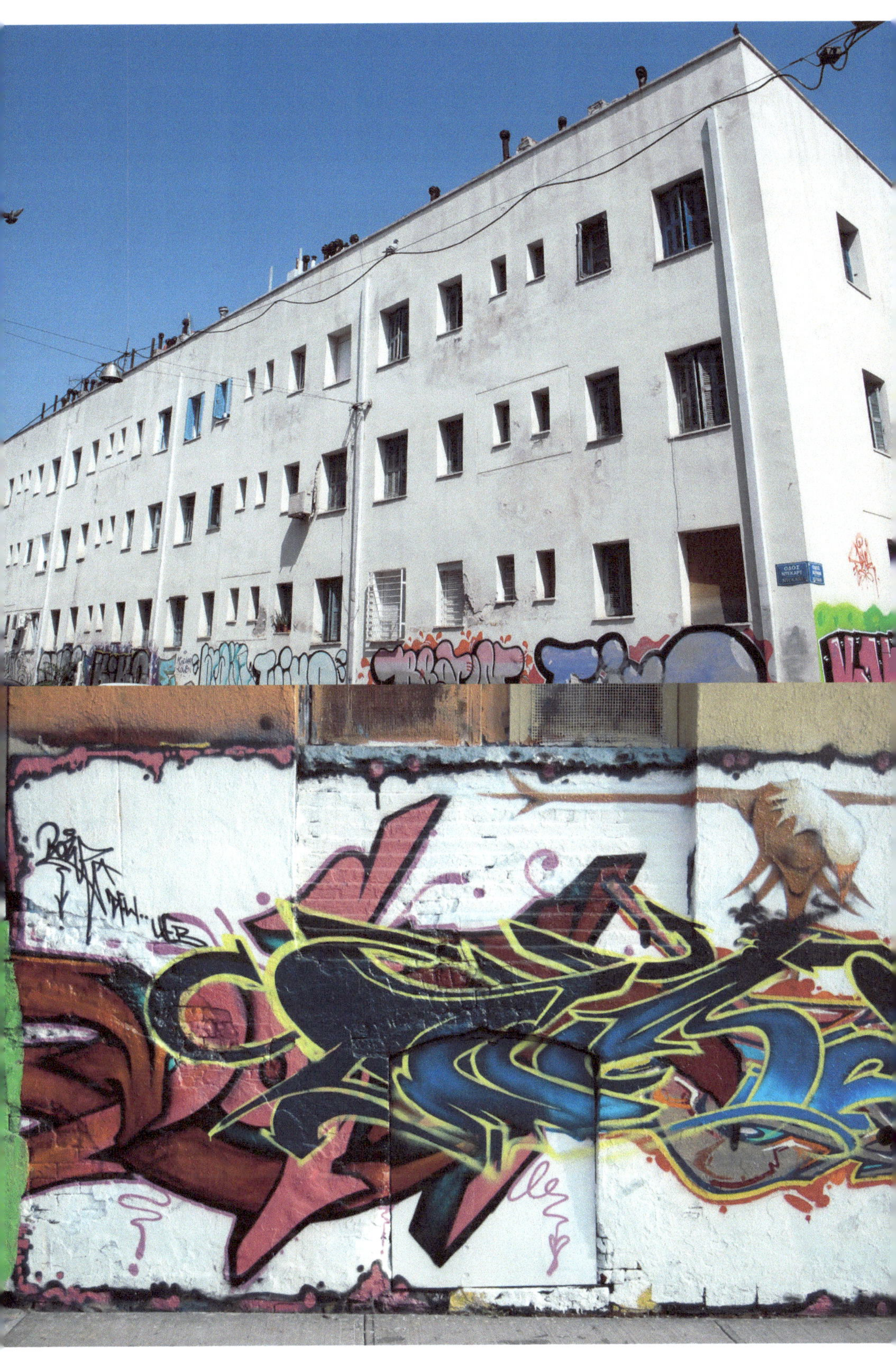
ΟΔΟΣ
ΝΤΕΚΑΡΥ

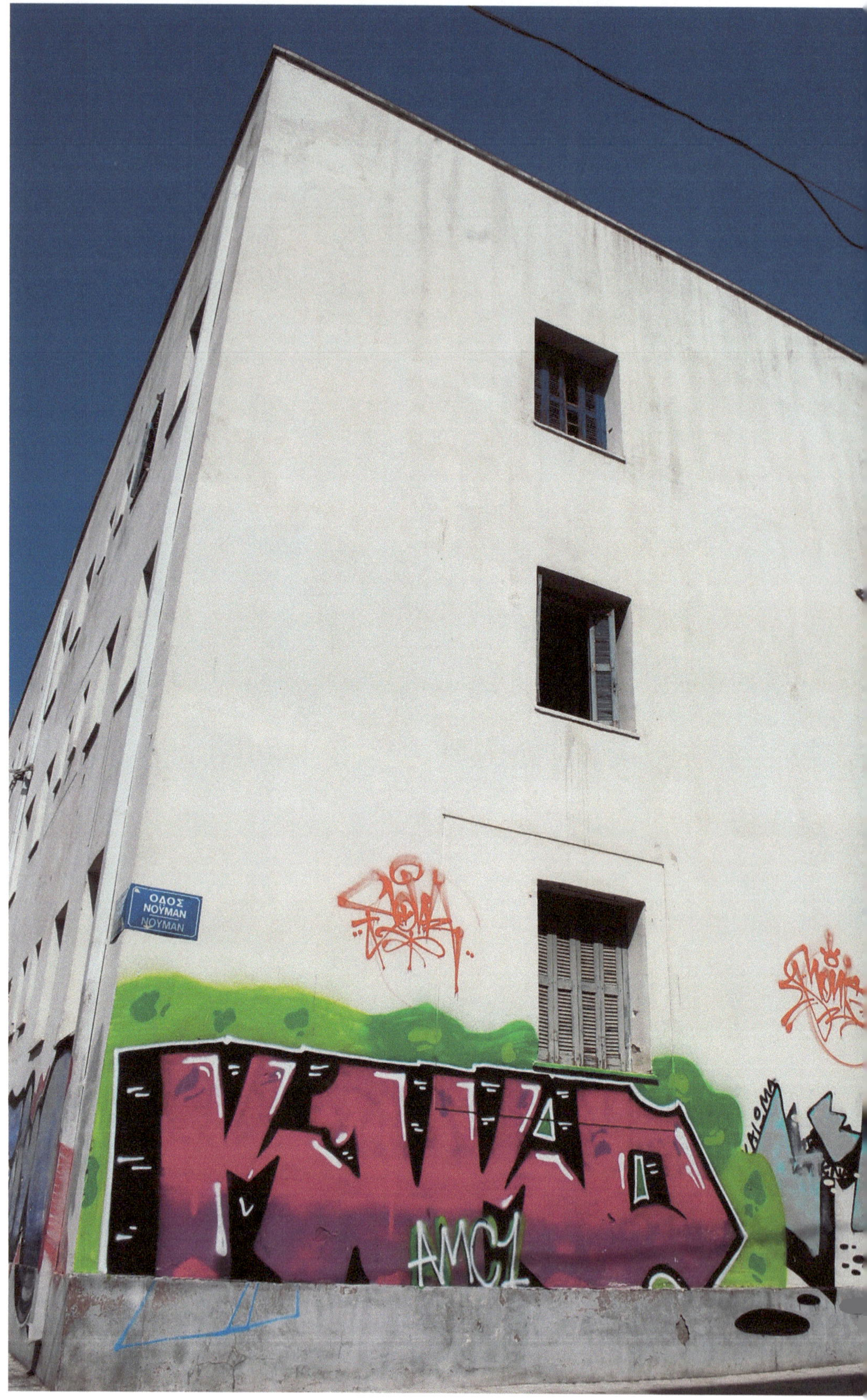
ΟΔΟΣ
ΝΟΫΜΑΝ
NOYMAN
AMC1

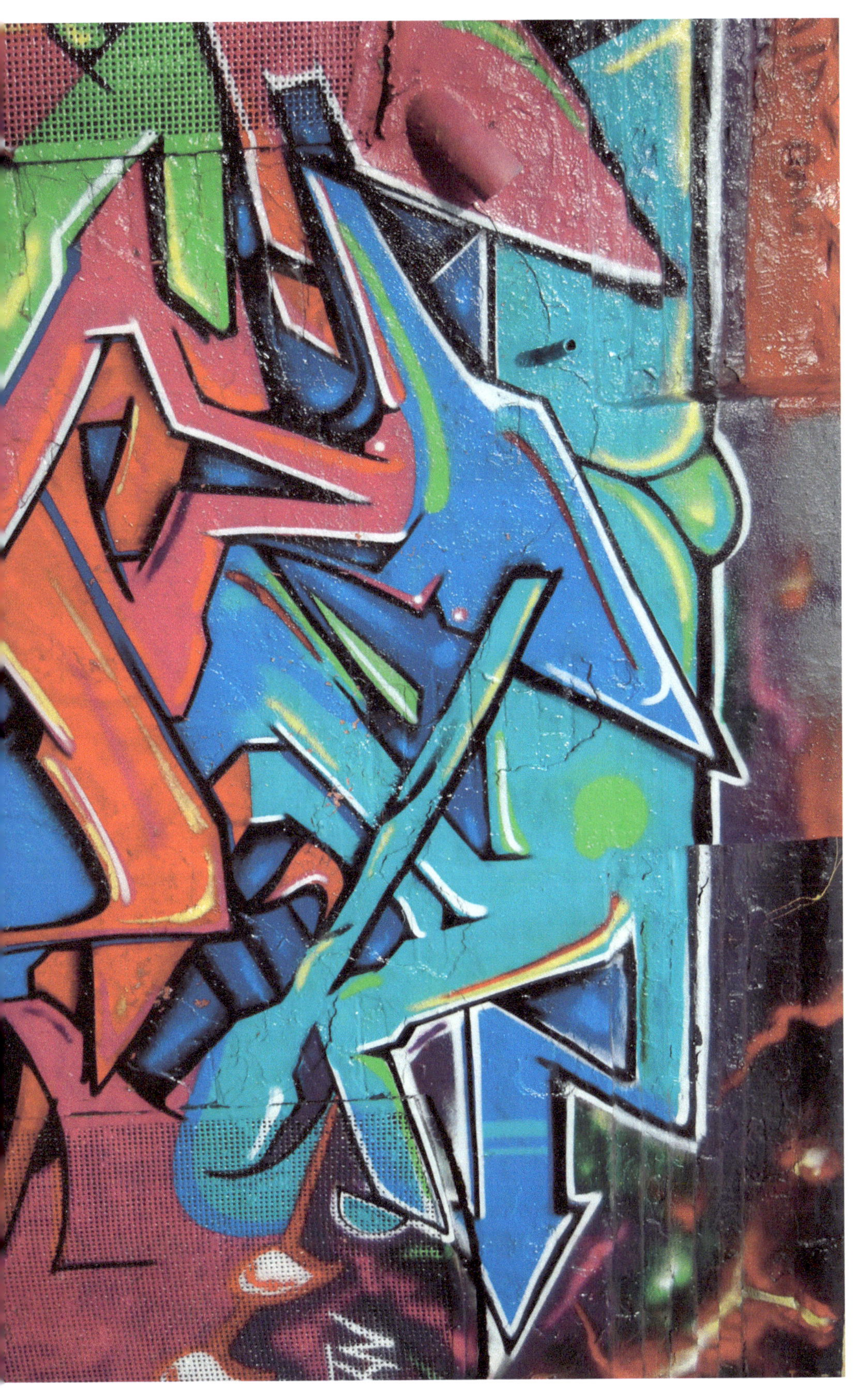

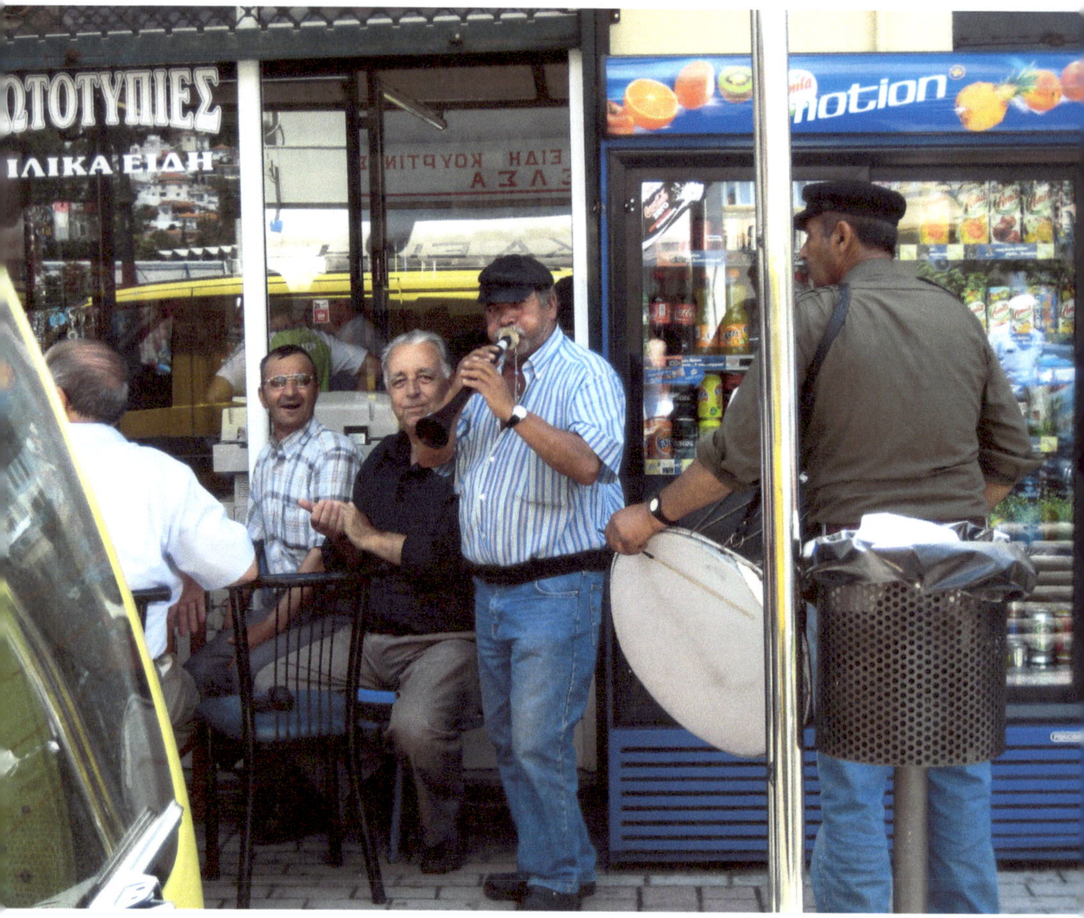

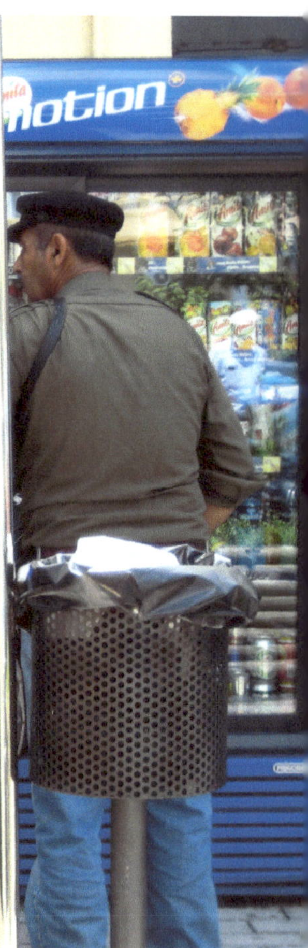

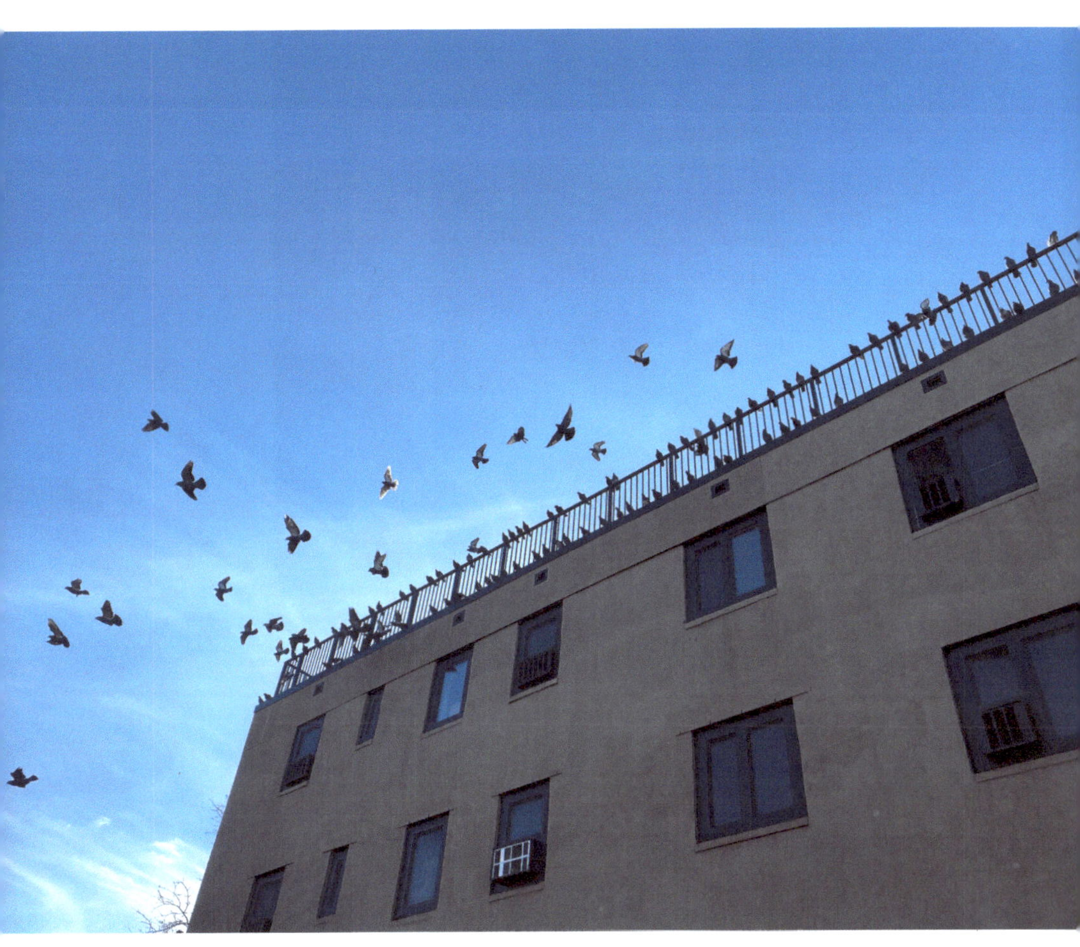

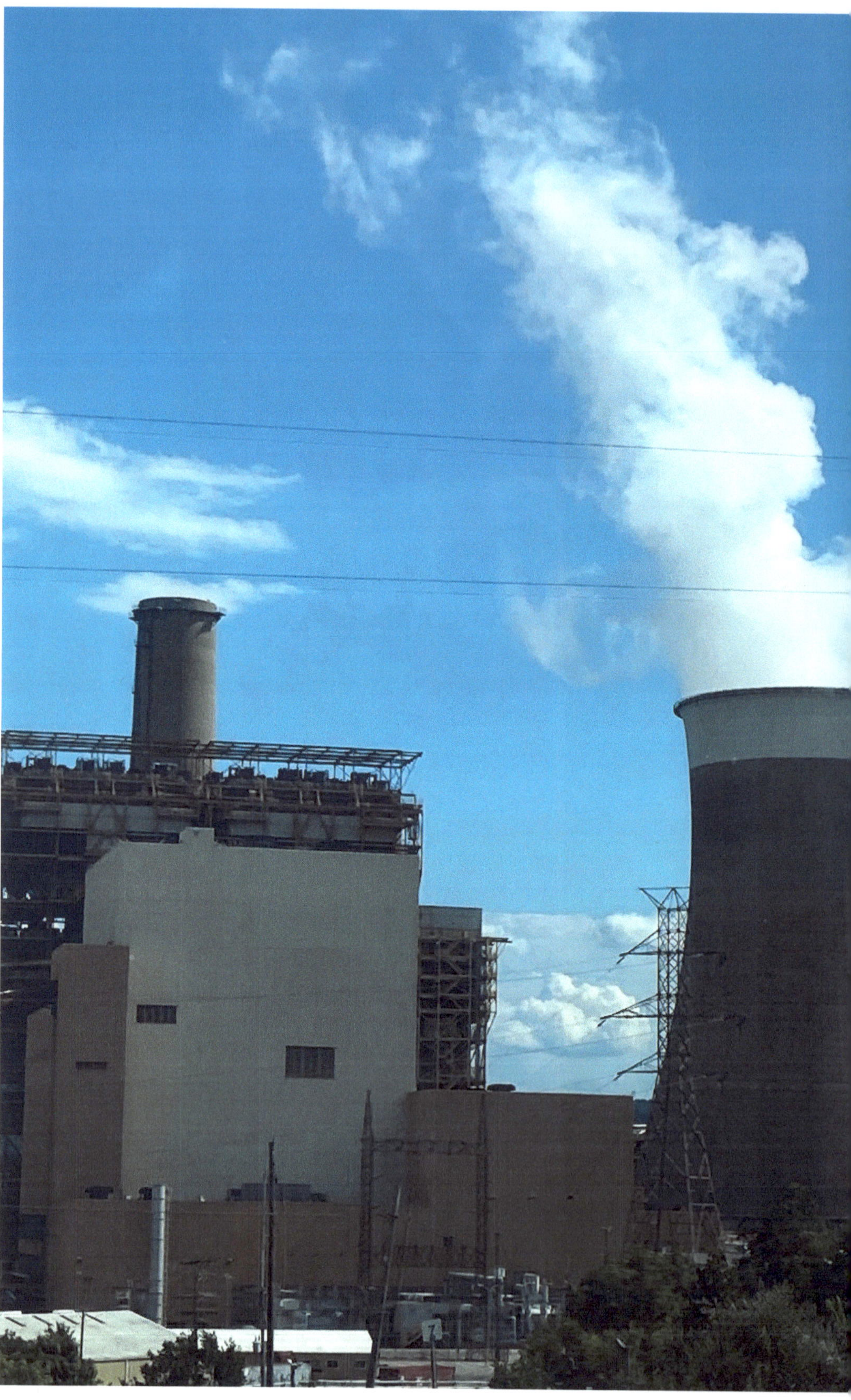

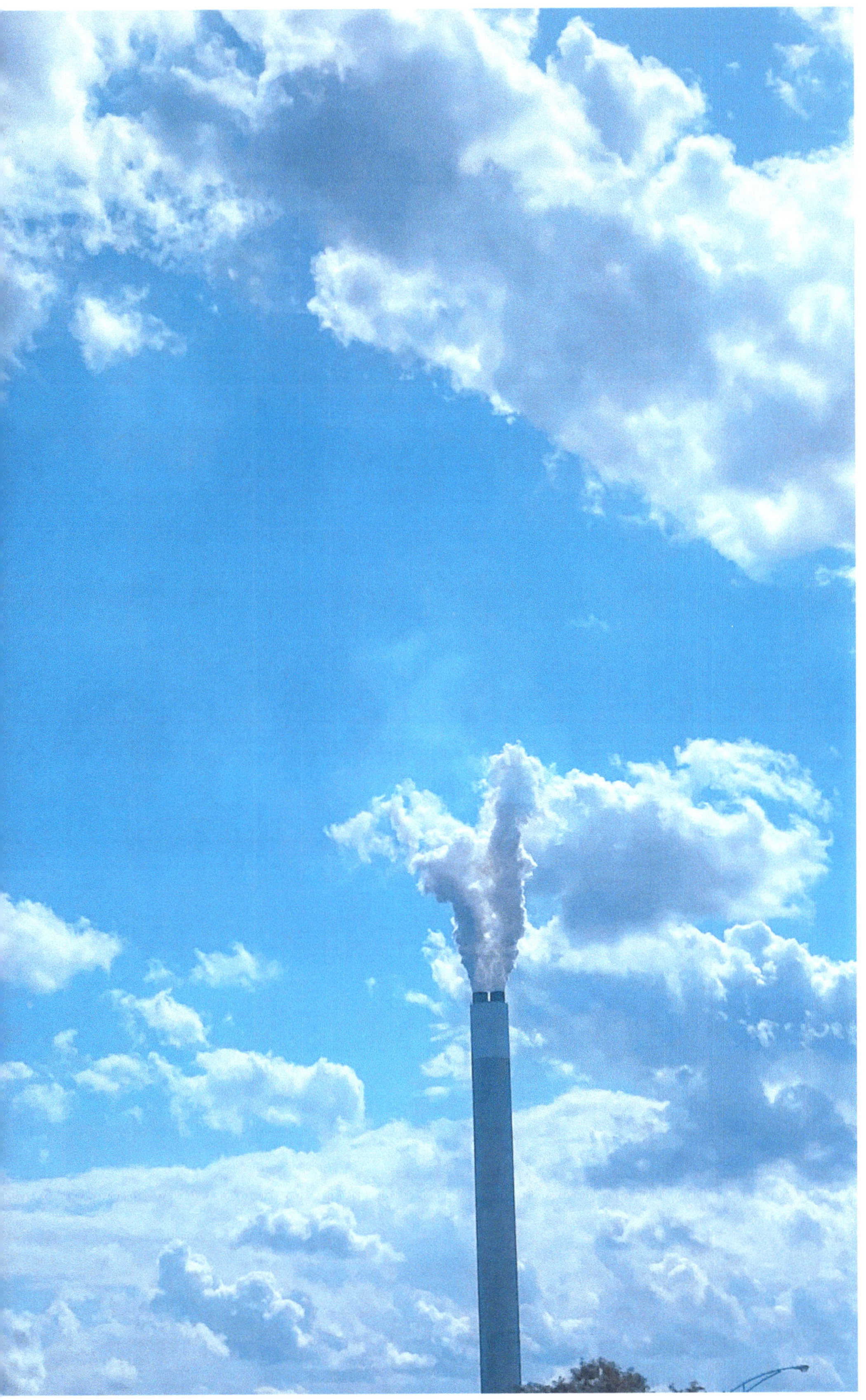

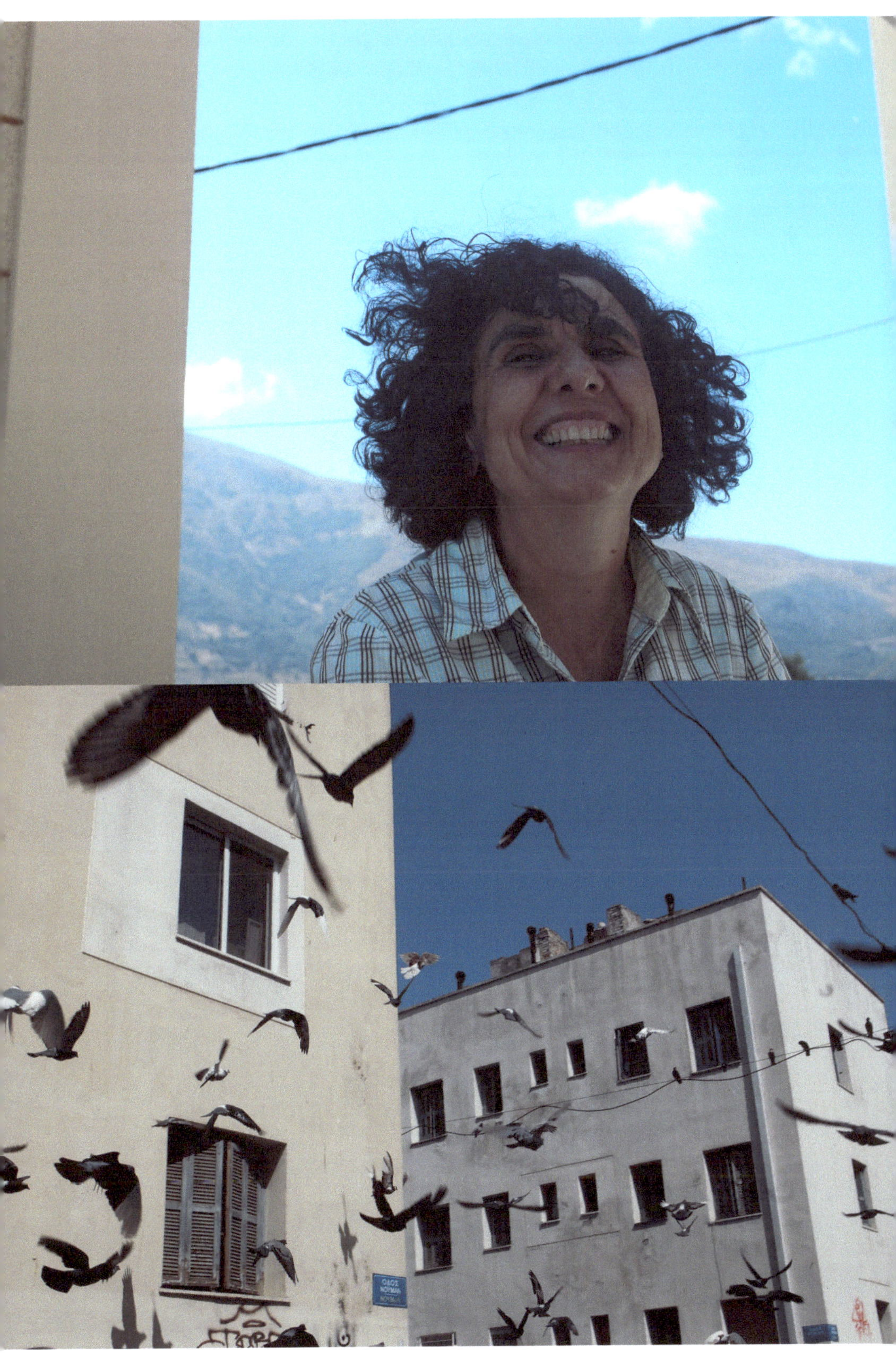

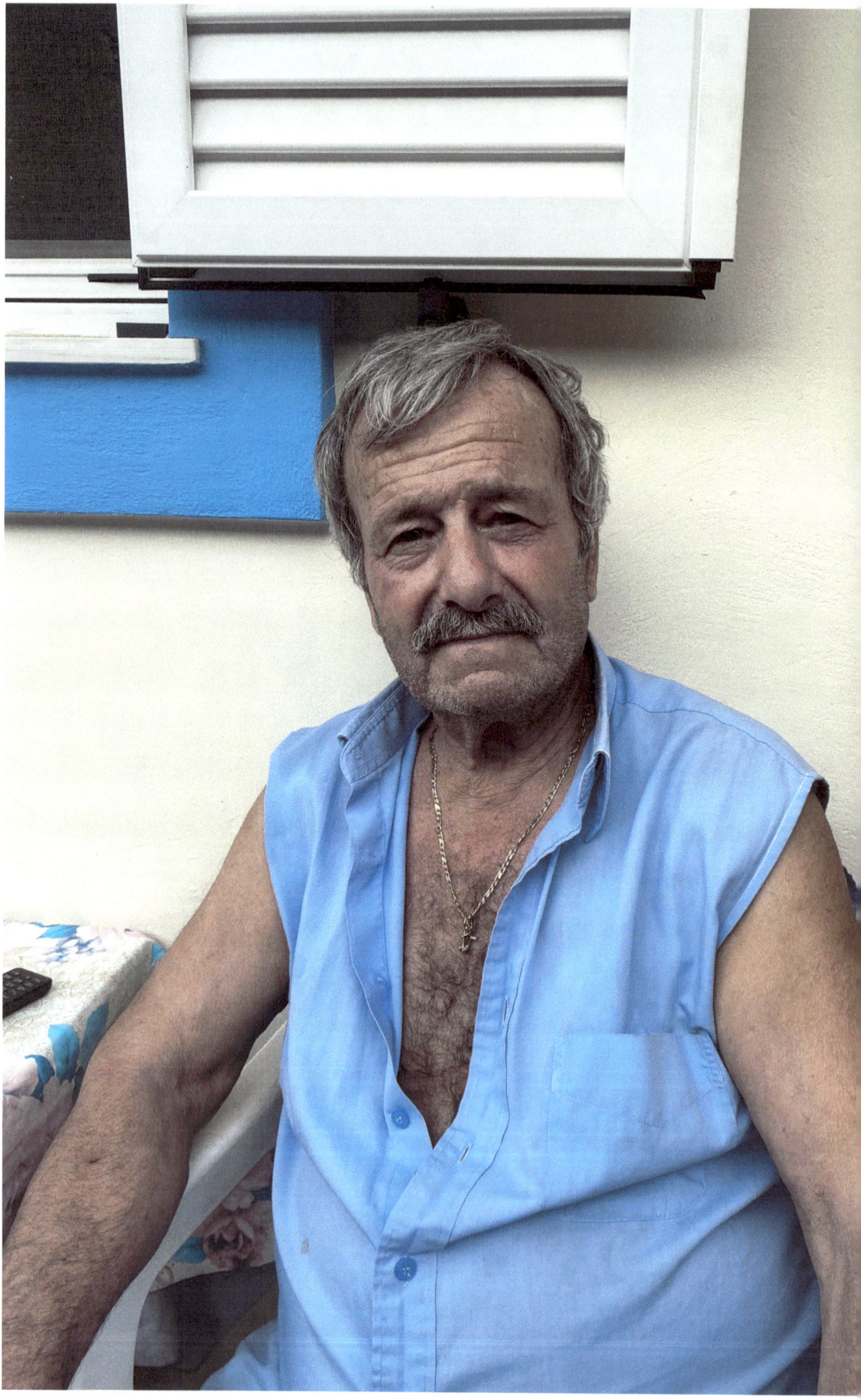

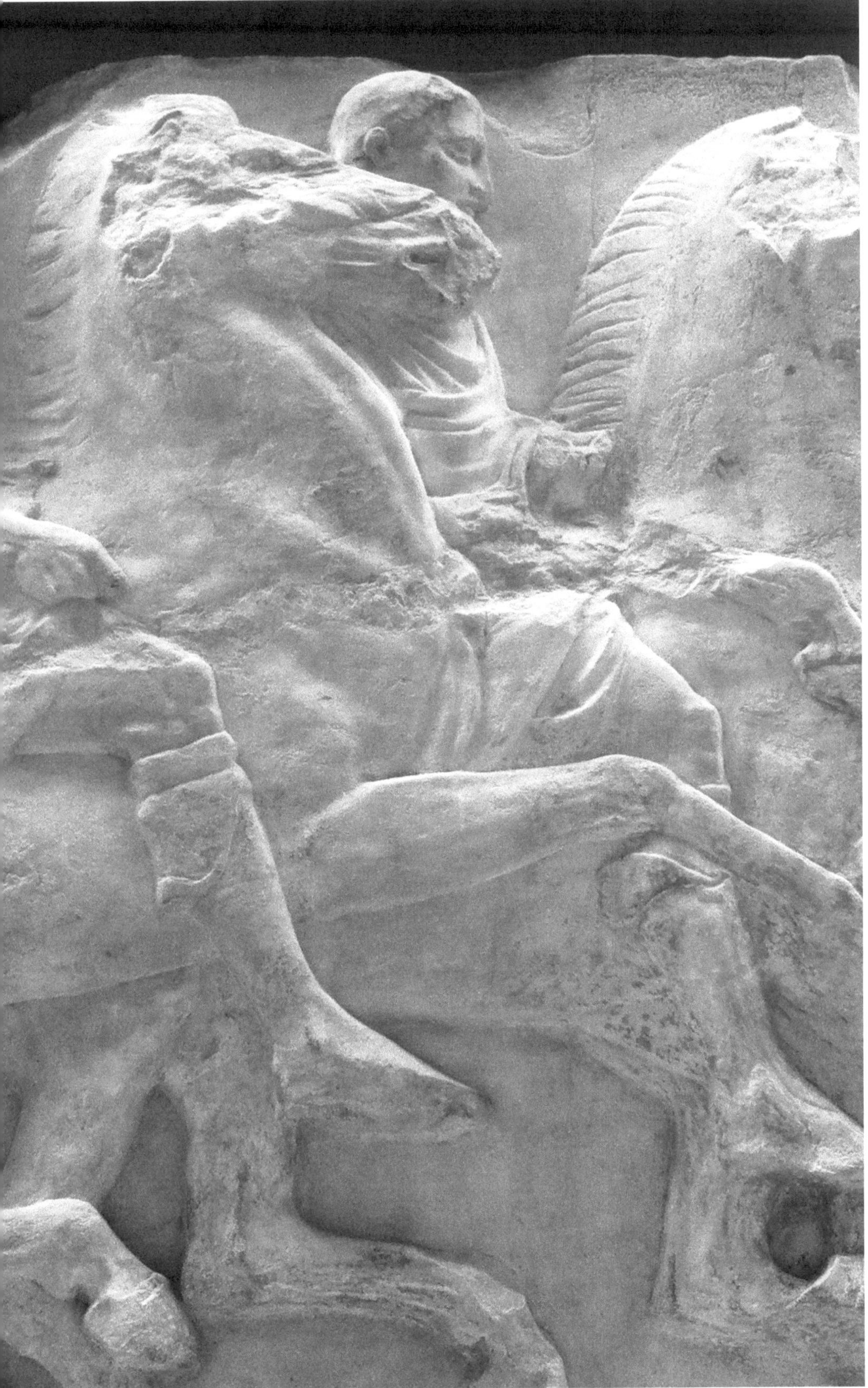

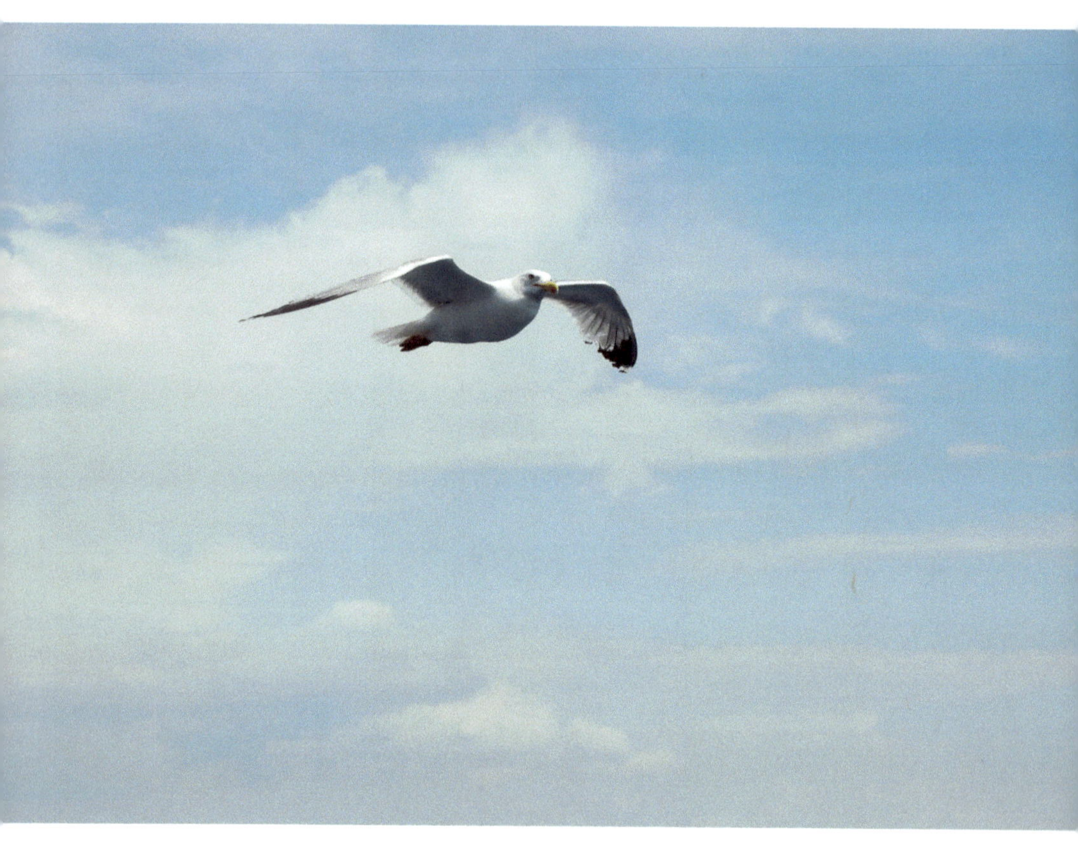

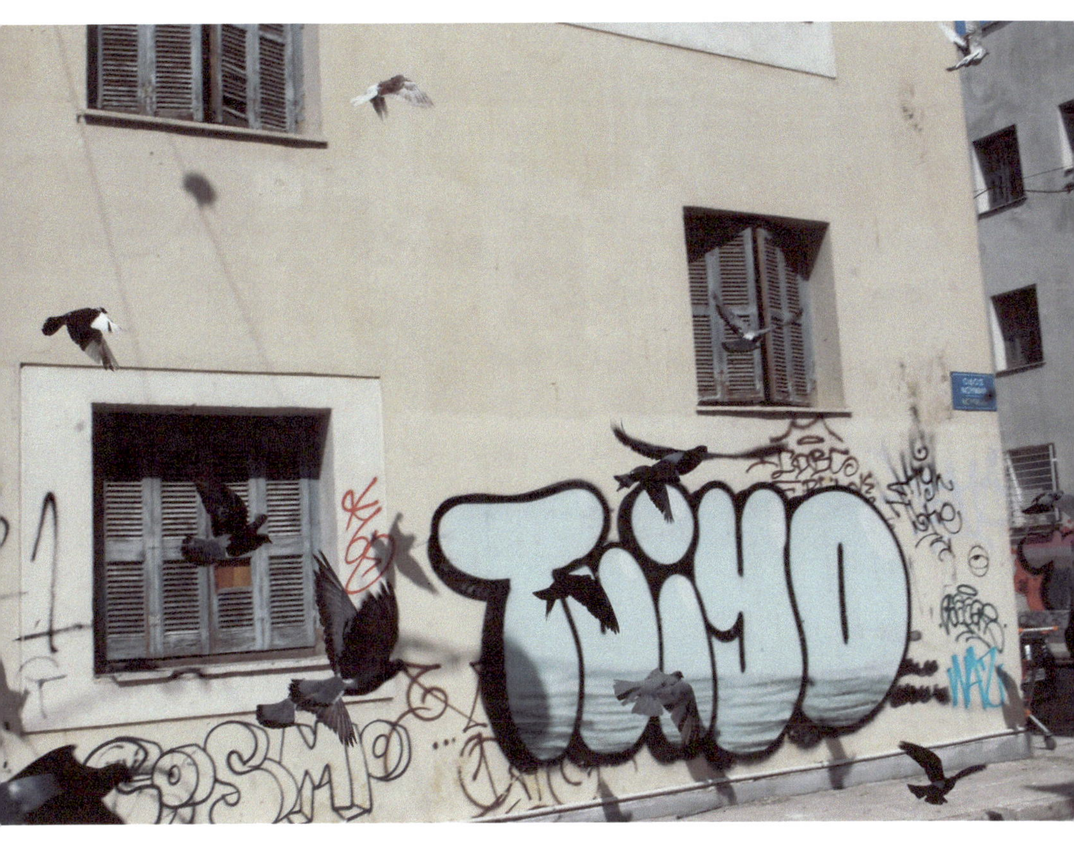

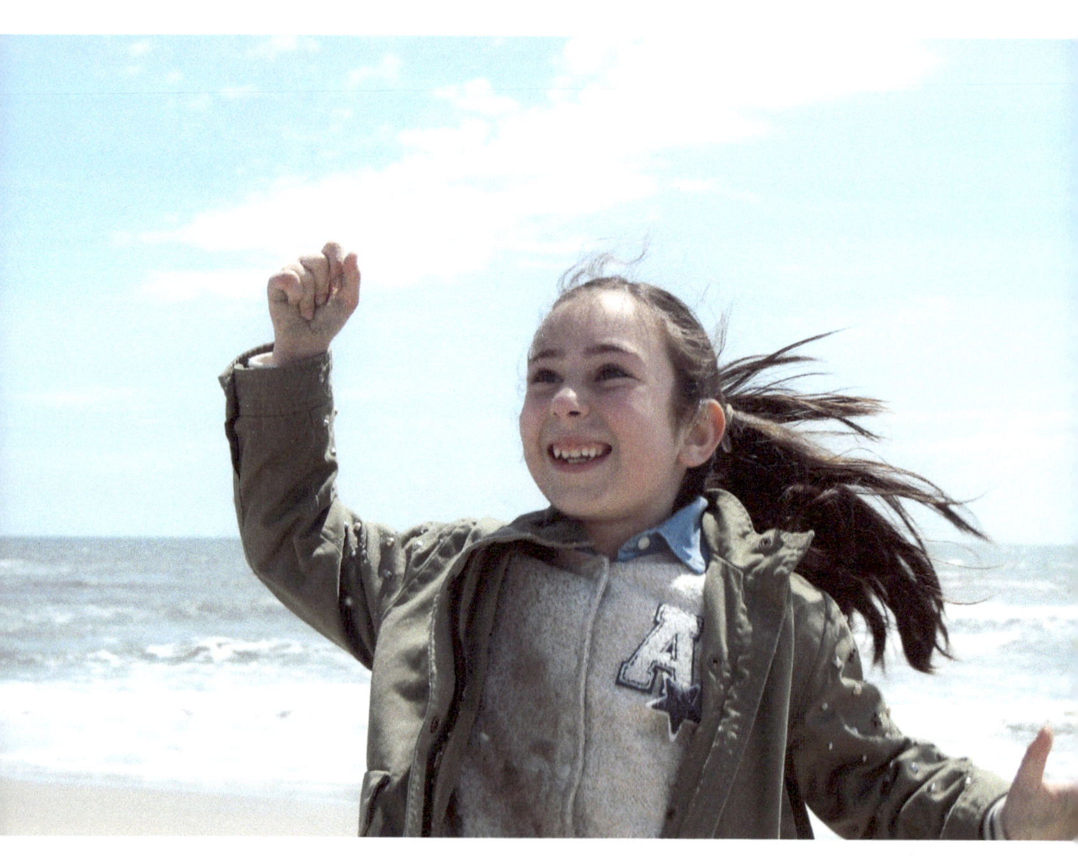

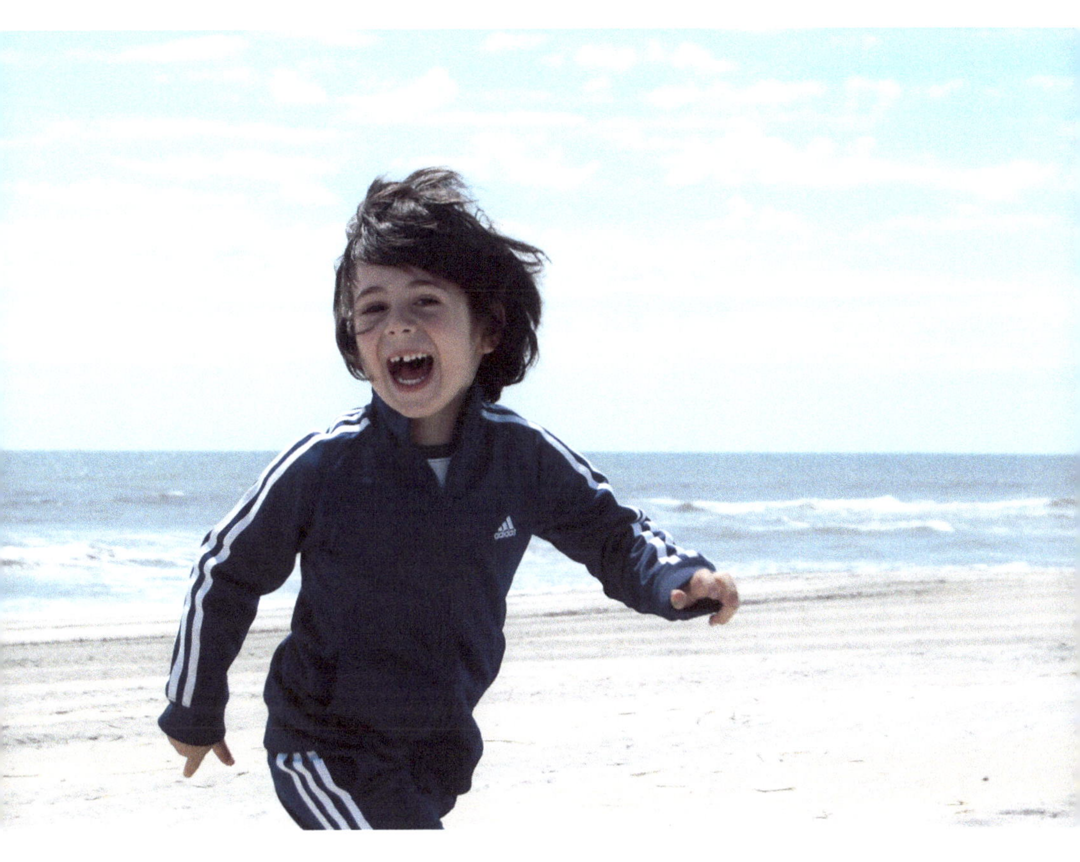

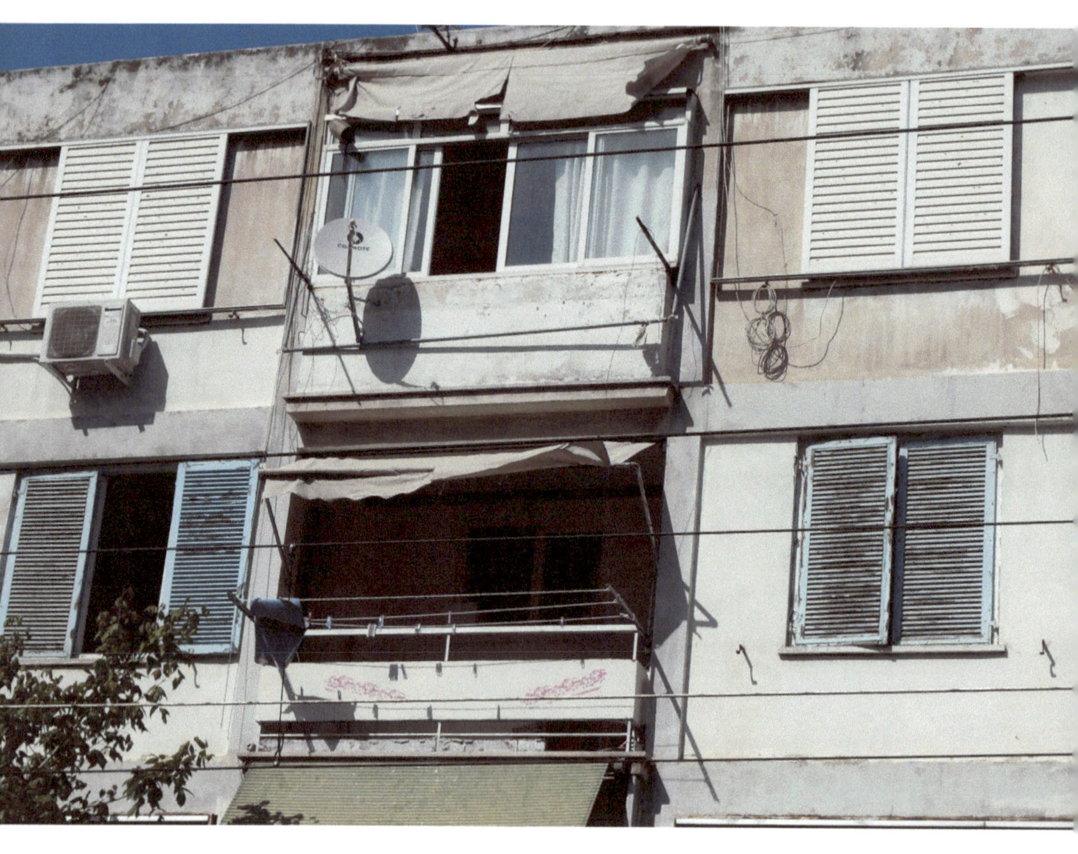

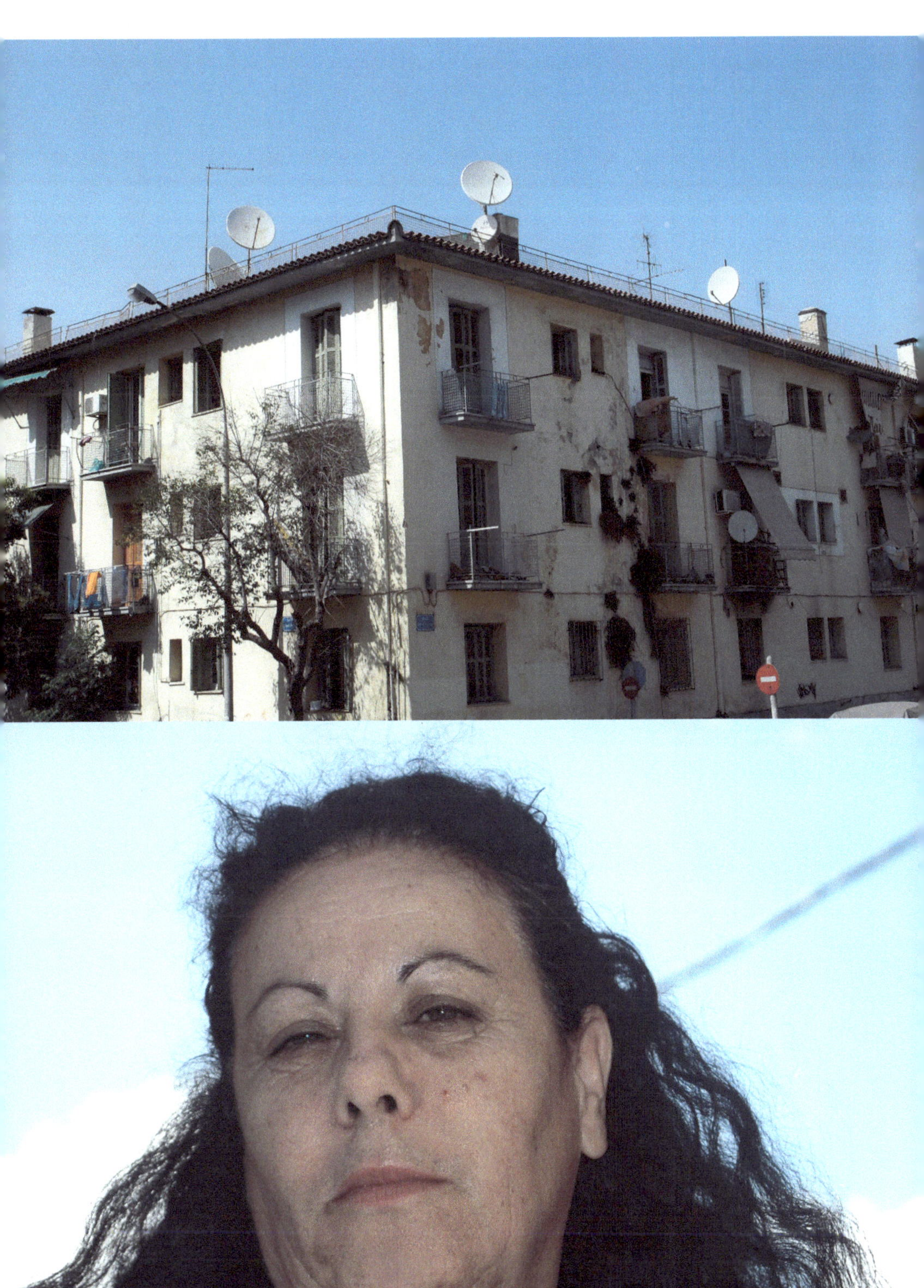

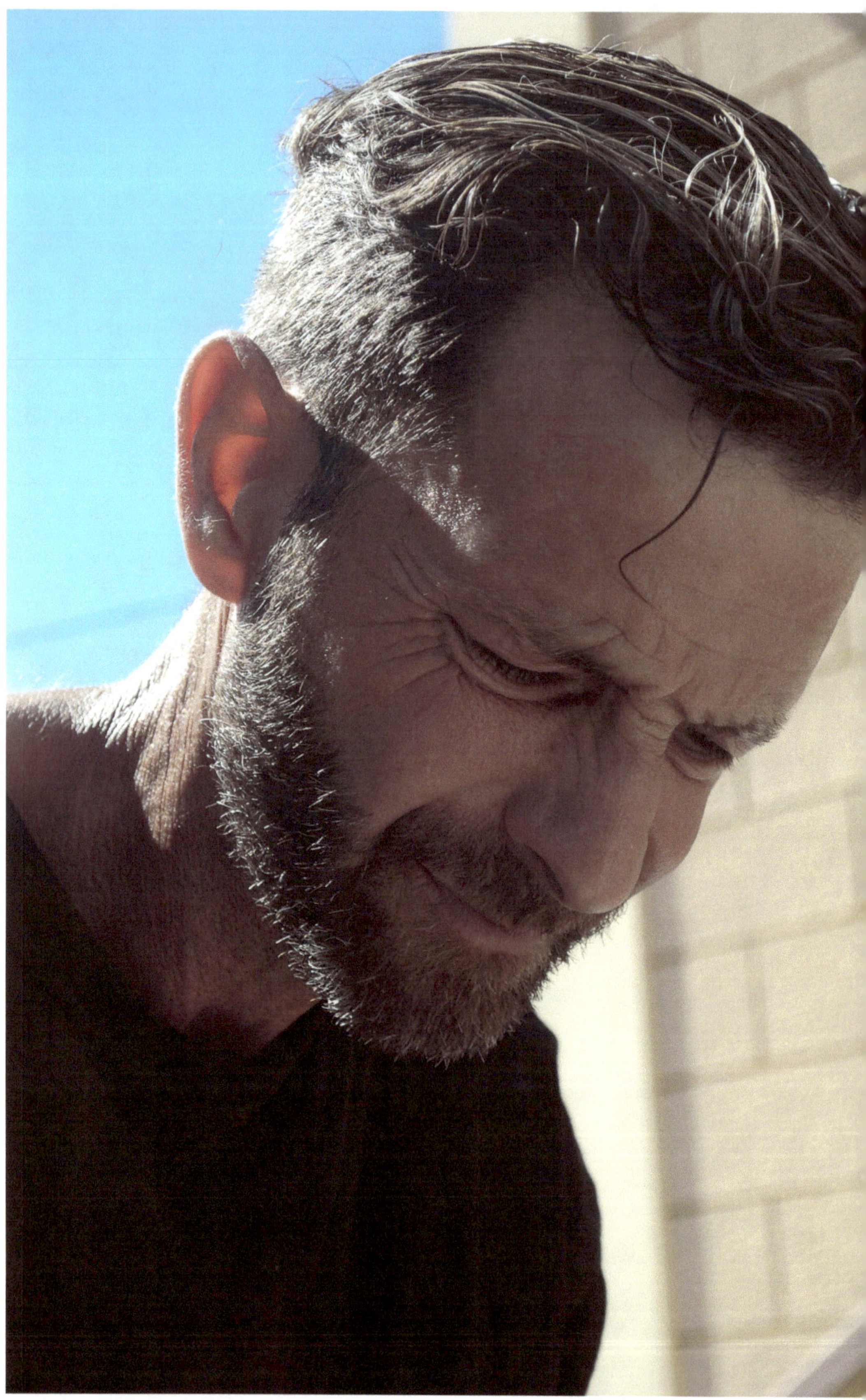

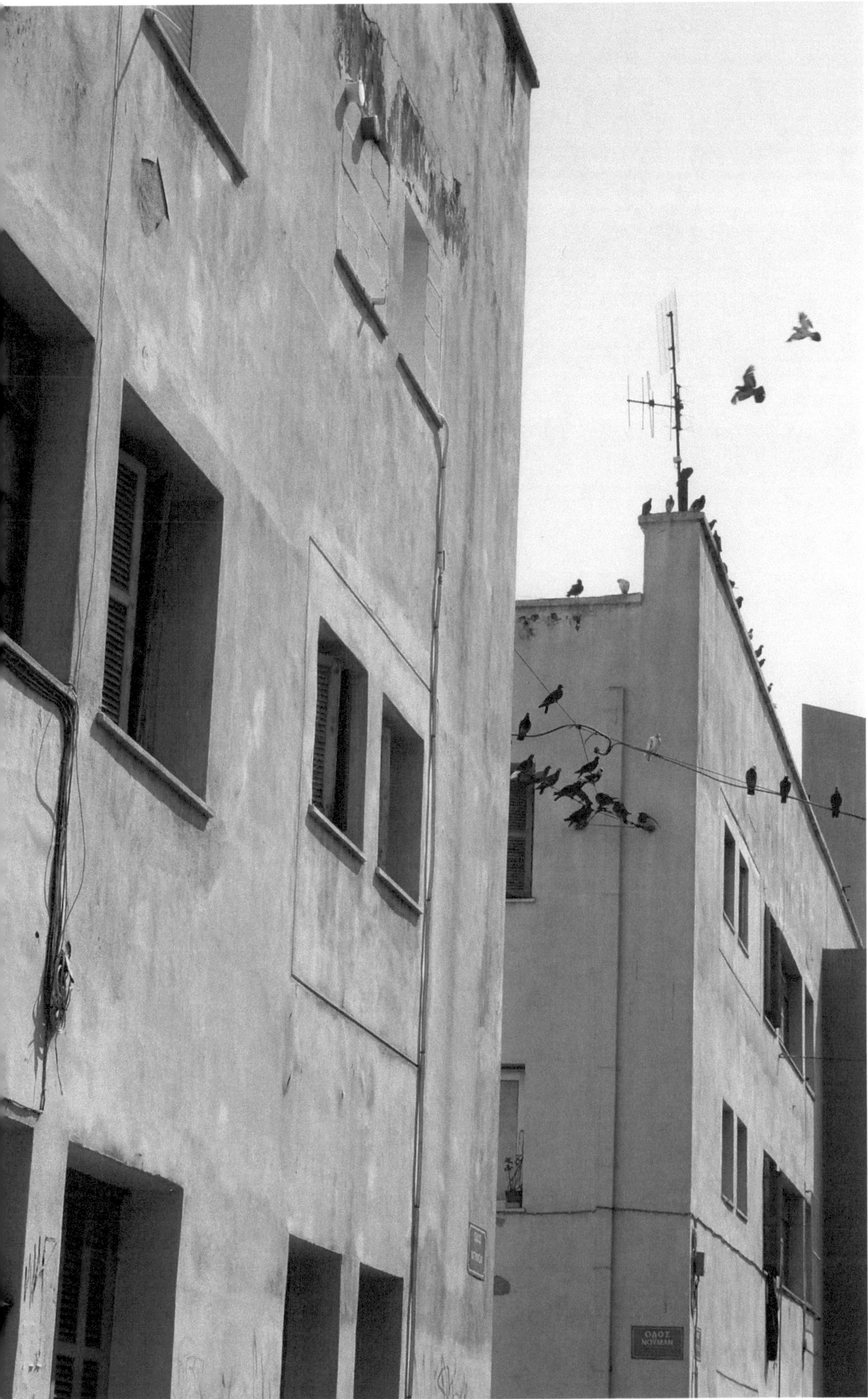
ΟΔΟΣ
ΝΟΥΜΑΝ

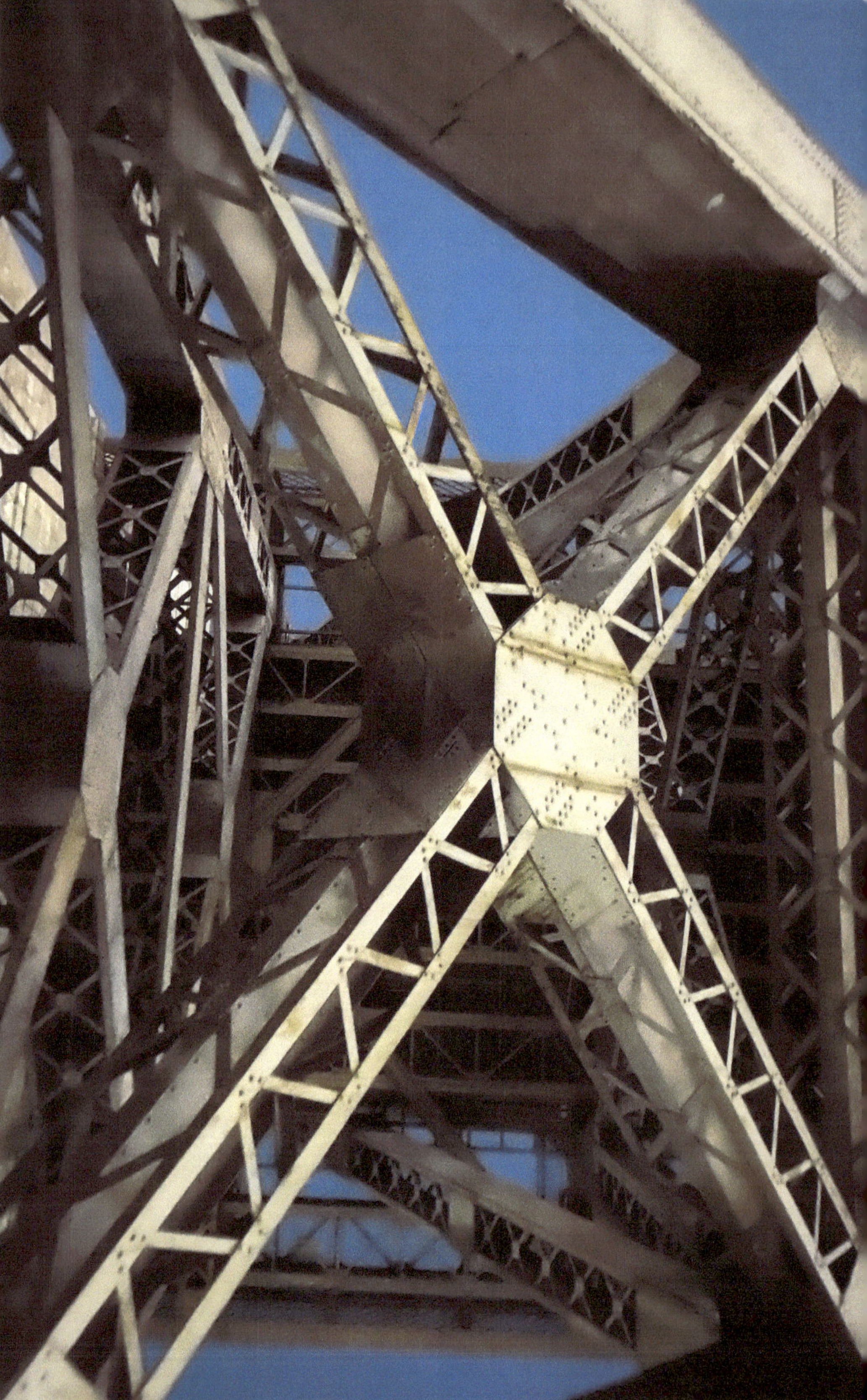

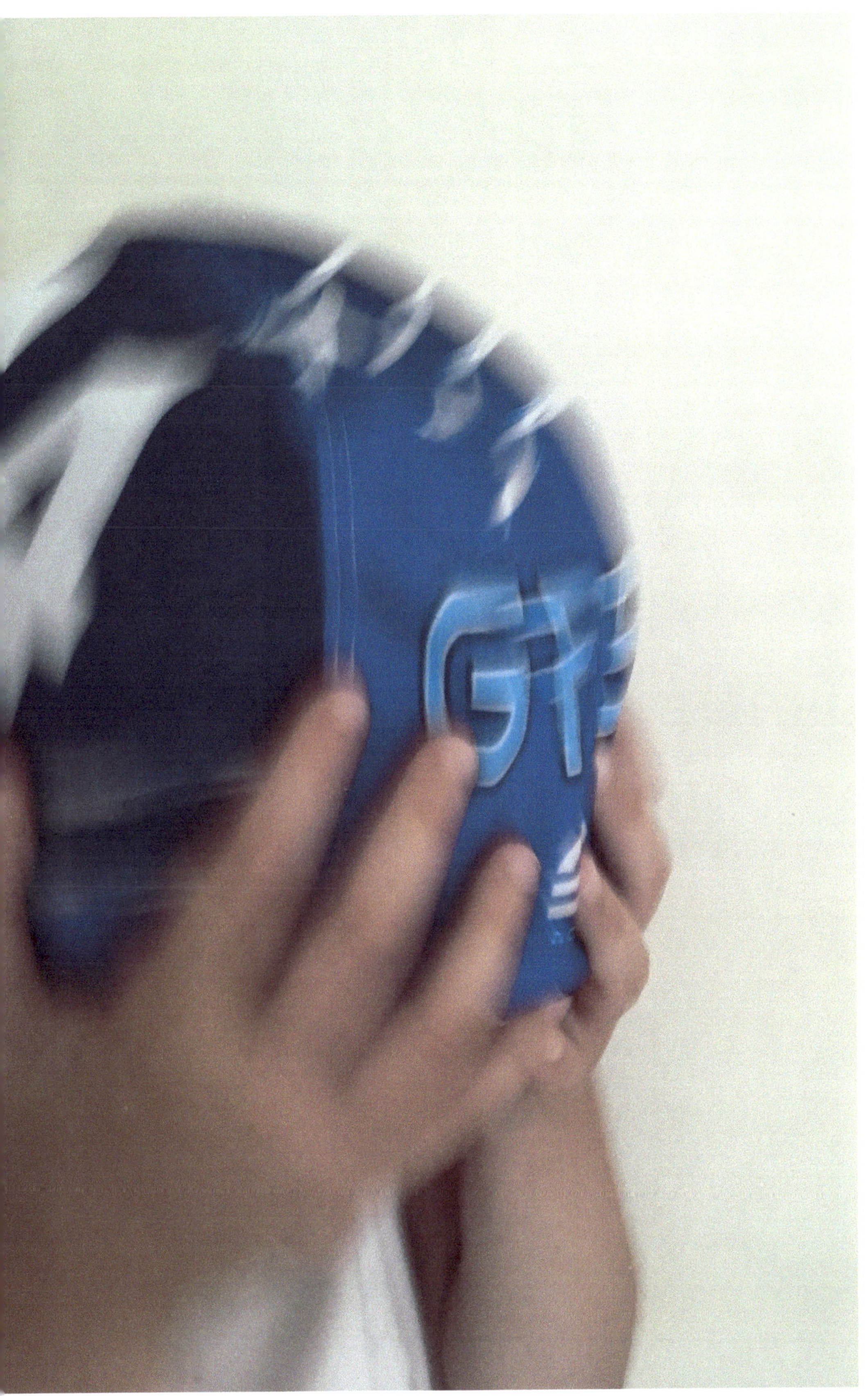

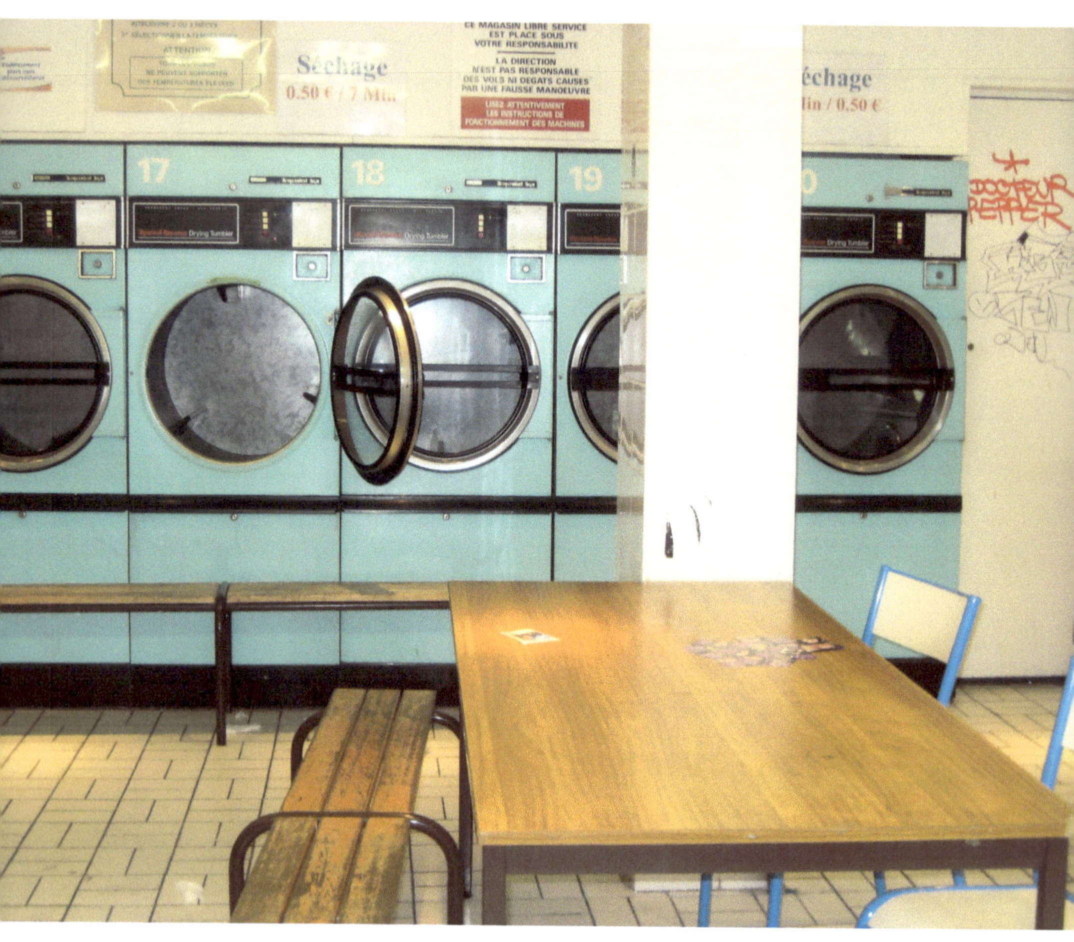
ATTENTION
NE PEUVENT SUPPORTER
DES TEMPERATURES ELEVEES
Séchage
0.50 € / 7 Min
CE MAGASIN LIBRE SERVICE
EST PLACE SOUS
VOTRE RESPONSABILITE
LA DIRECTION
N'EST PAS RESPONSABLE
DES VOLS NI DEGATS CAUSES
PAR UNE FAUSSE MANOEUVRE
LISEZ ATTENTIVEMENT
LES INSTRUCTIONS DE
FONCTIONNEMENT DES MACHINES
17
18
19
Drying Tumbler
échage
Min / 0,50 €
DOCTEUR
PEPPER

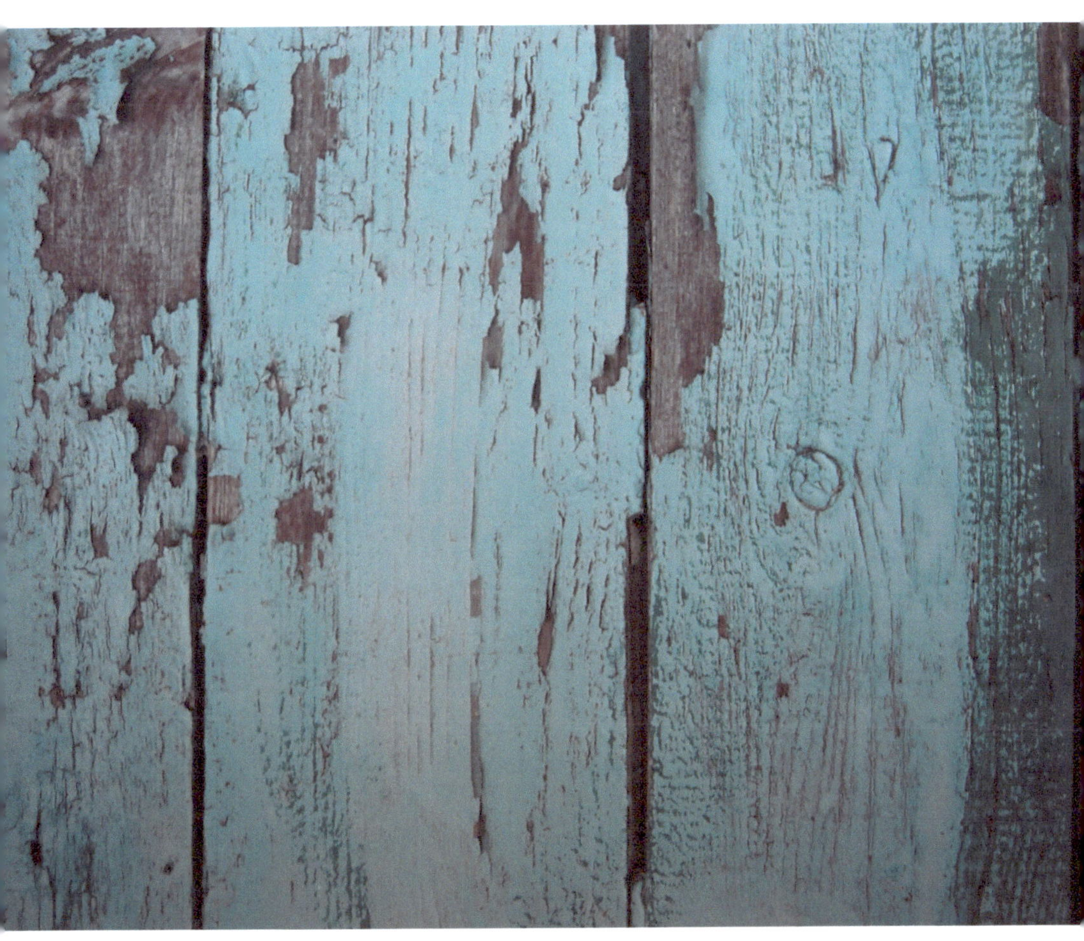

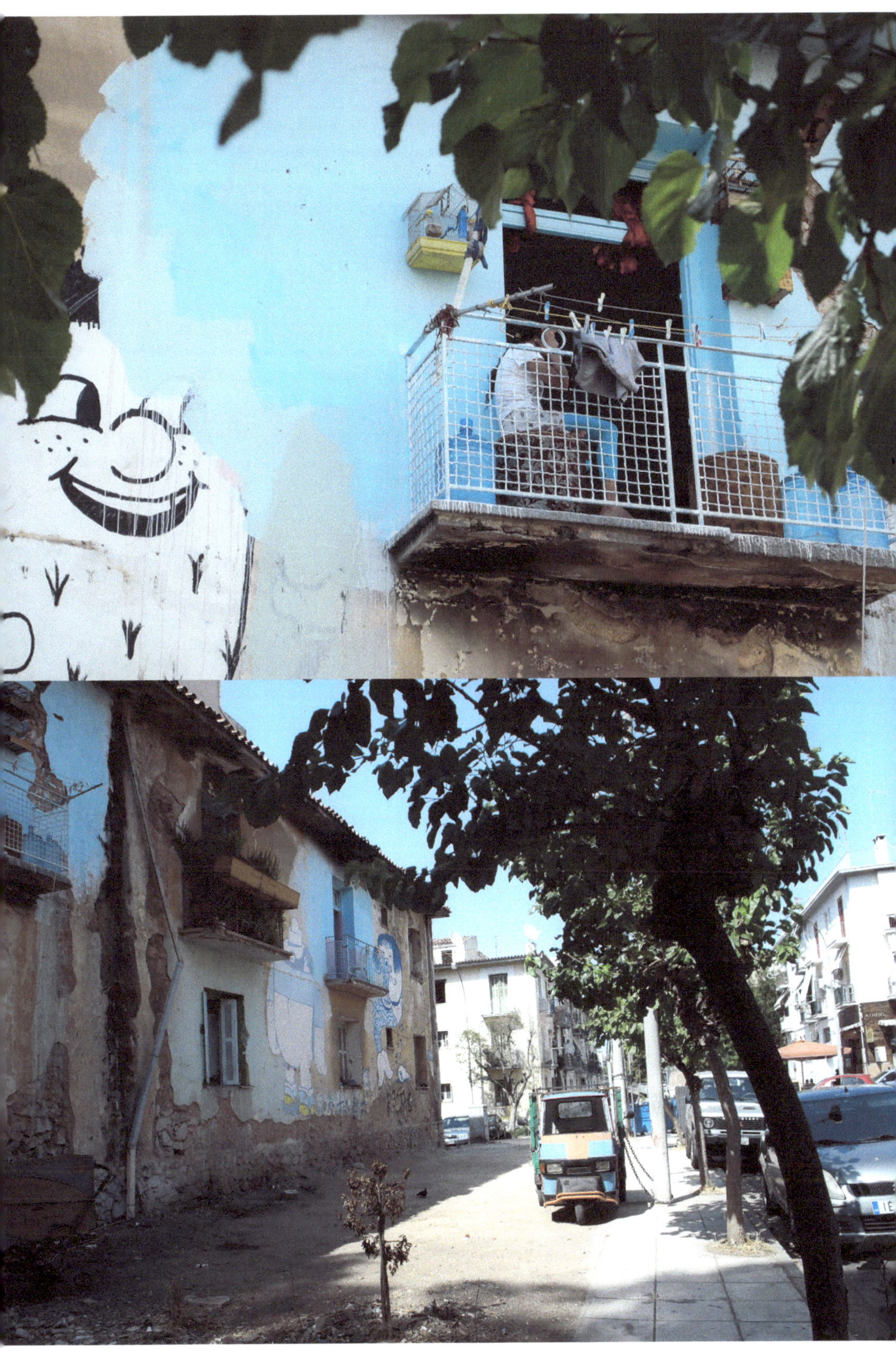

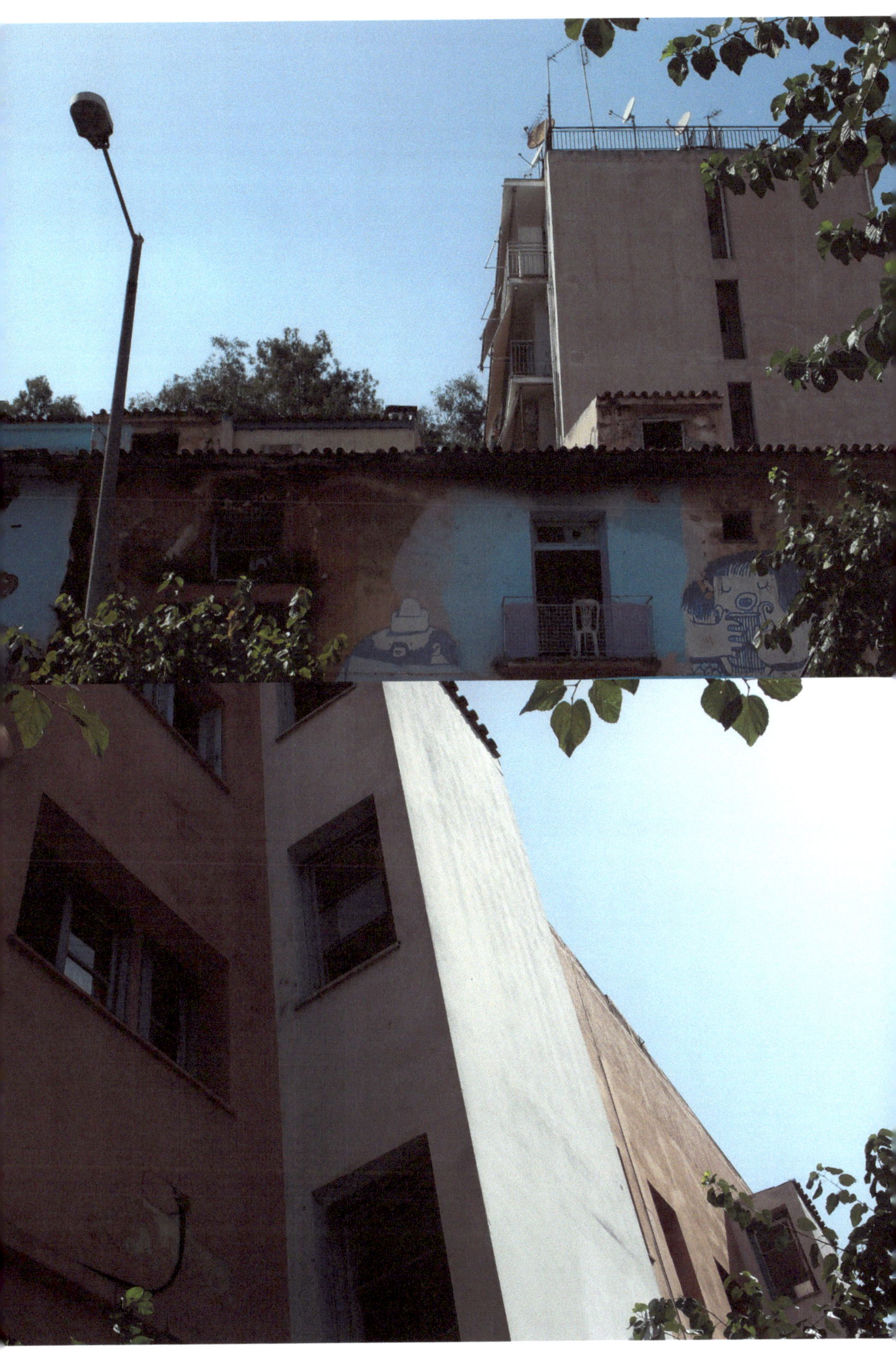

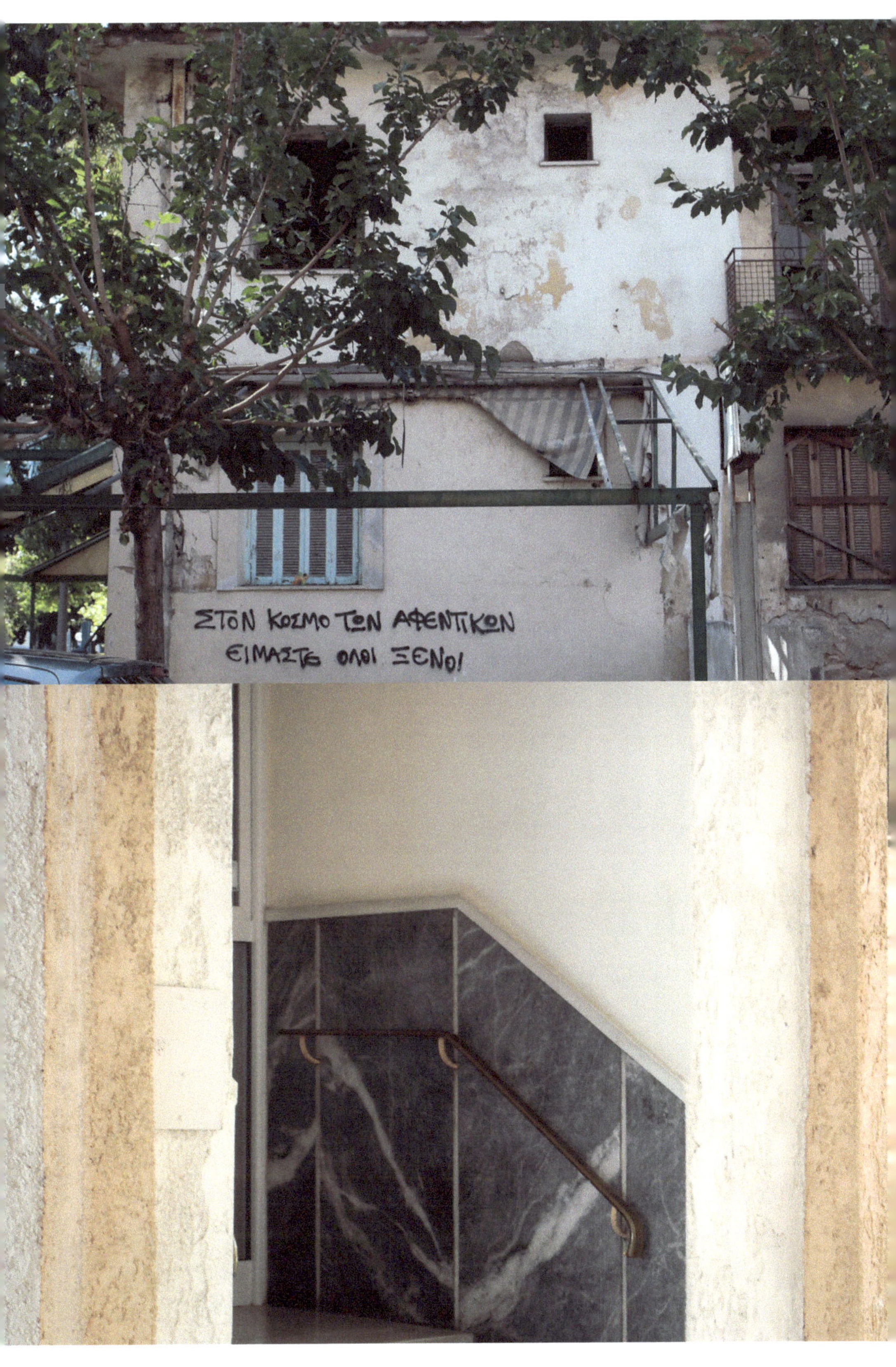
ΣΤΟΝ ΚΟΣΜΟ ΤΩΝ ΑΦΕΝΤΙΚΩΝ
ΕΙΜΑΣΤΕ ΟΛΟΙ ΞΕΝΟΙ!

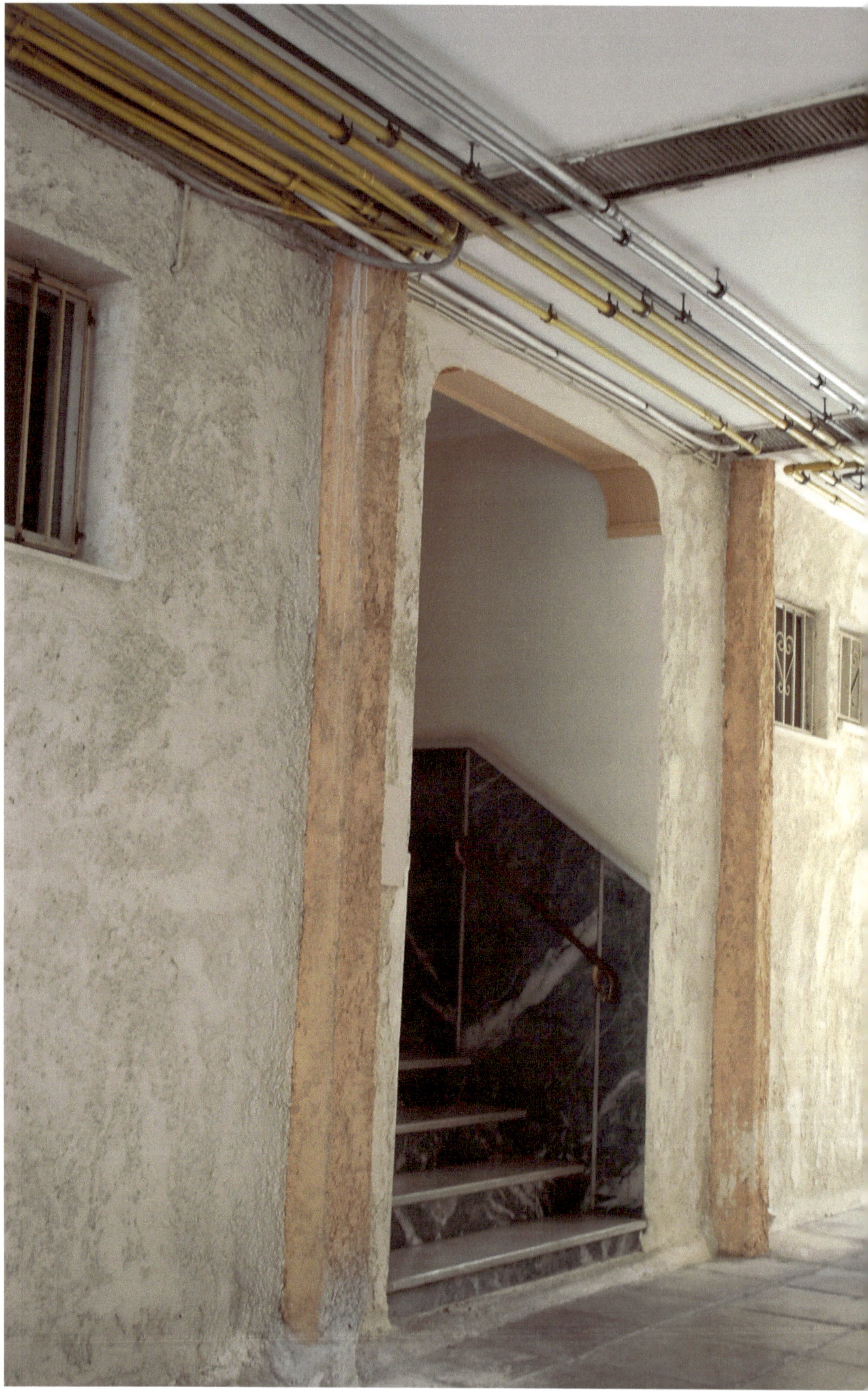

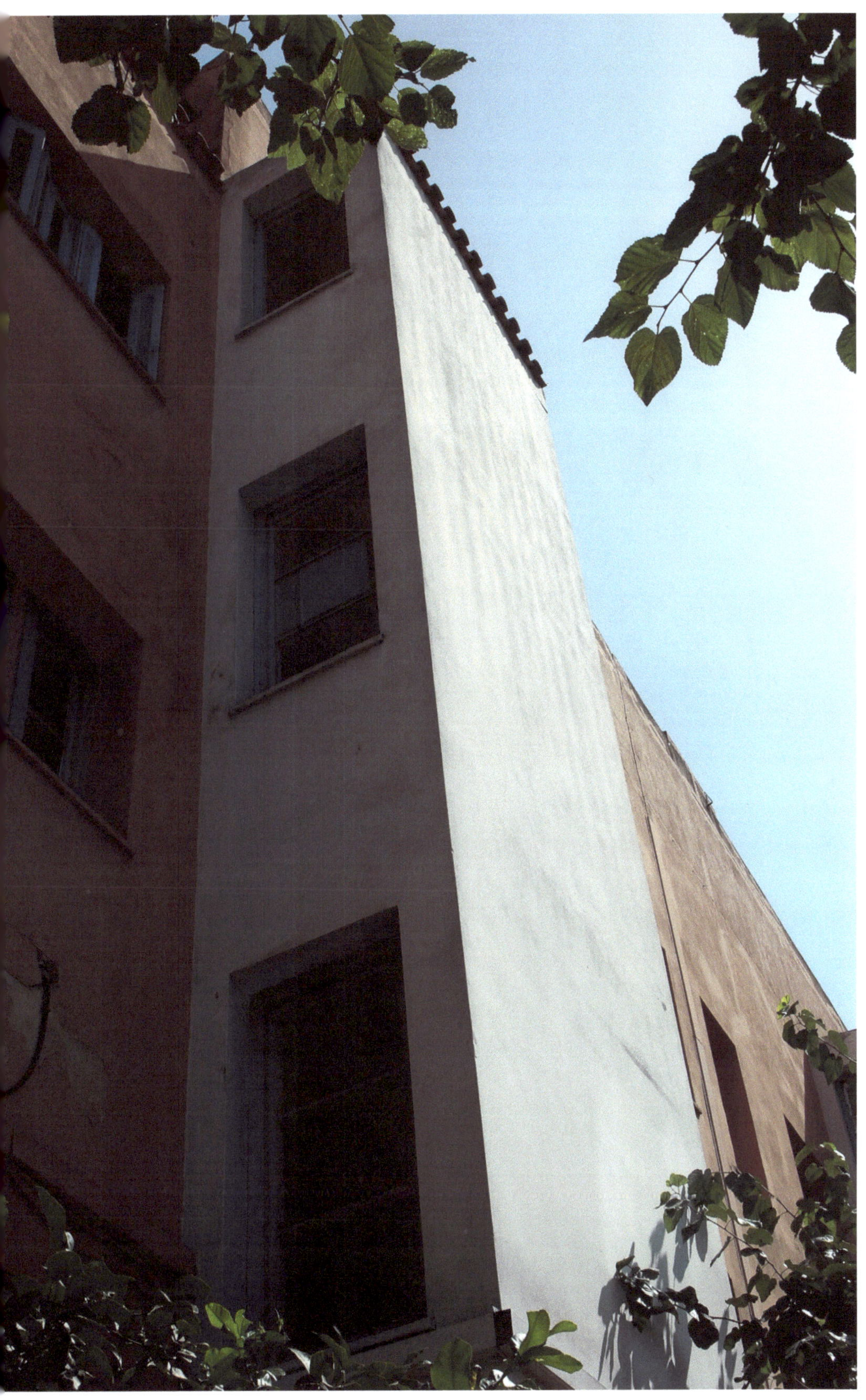

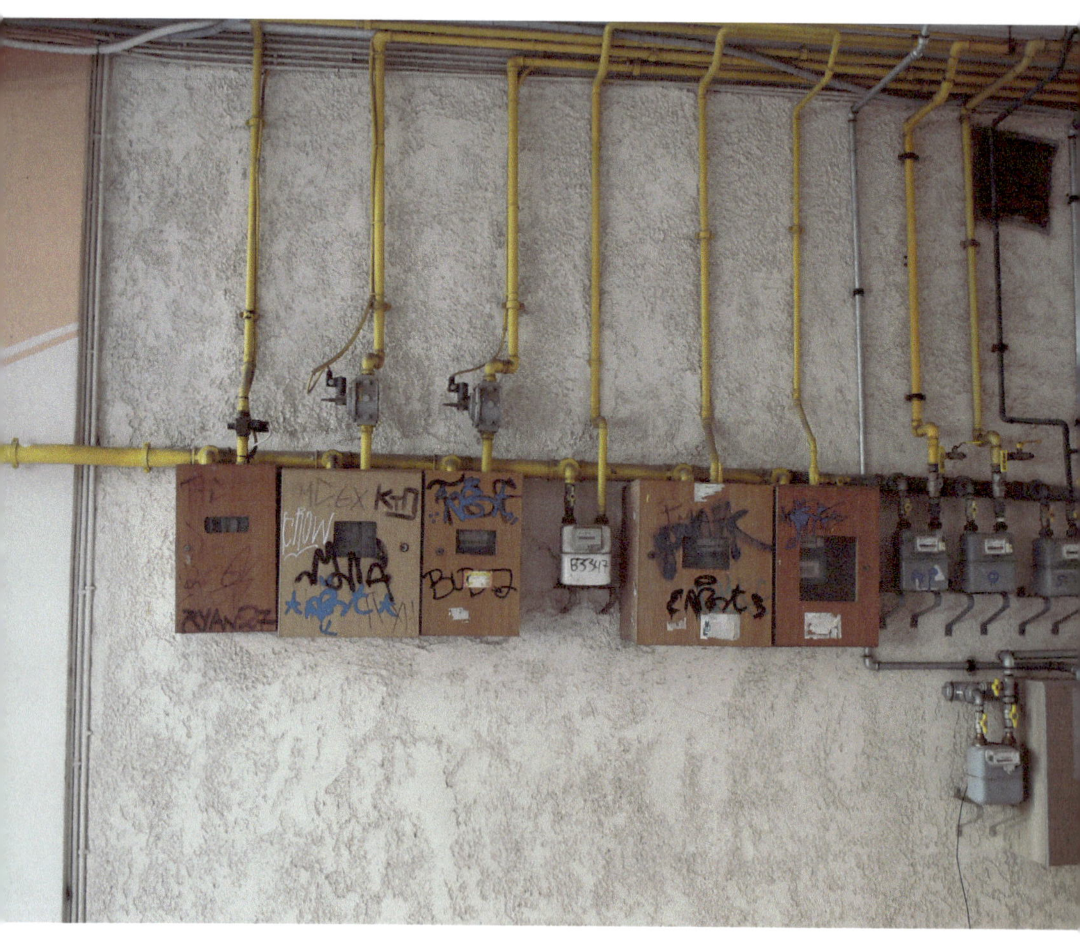

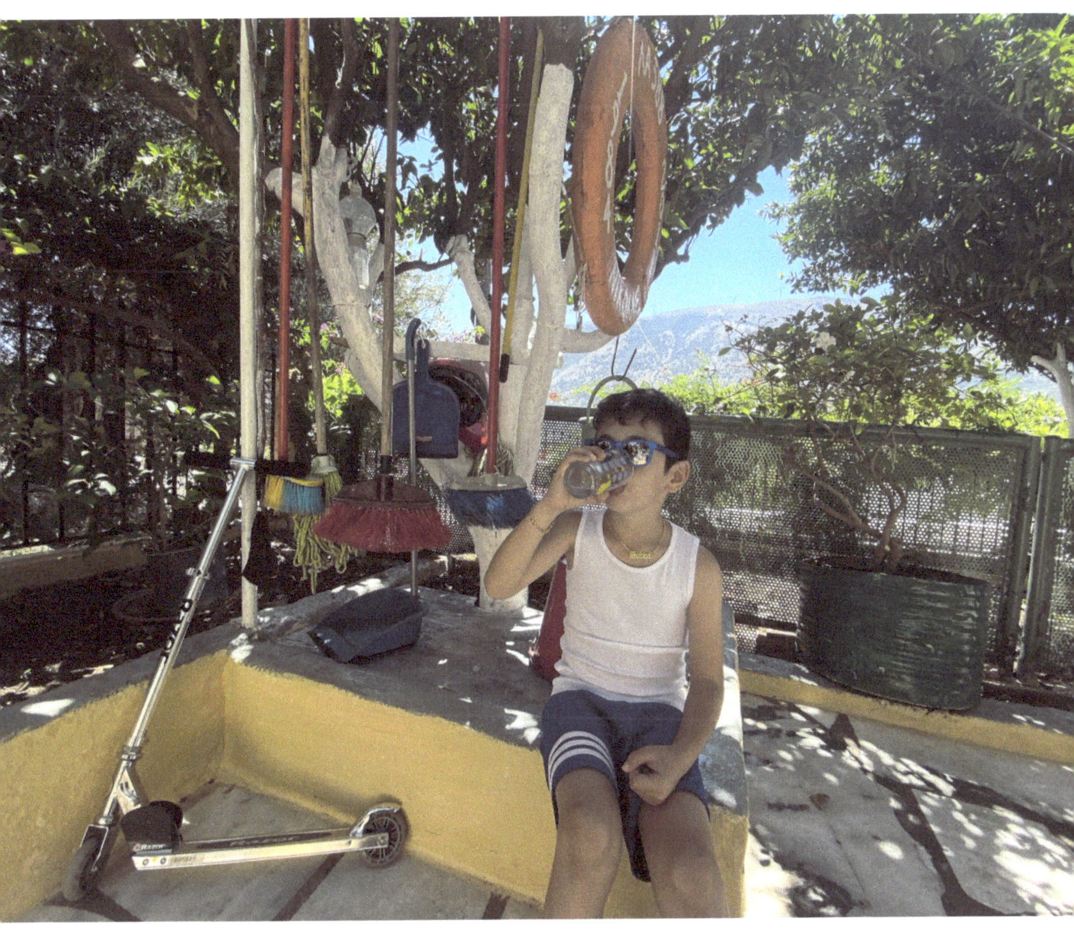

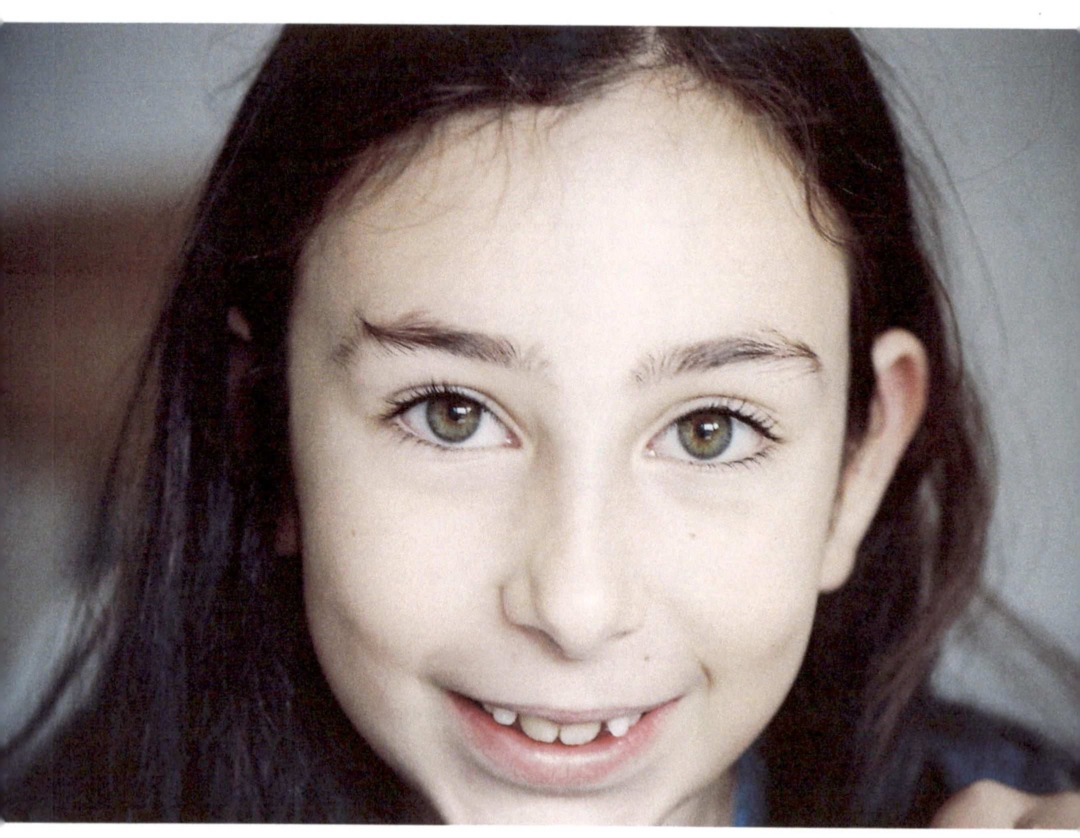

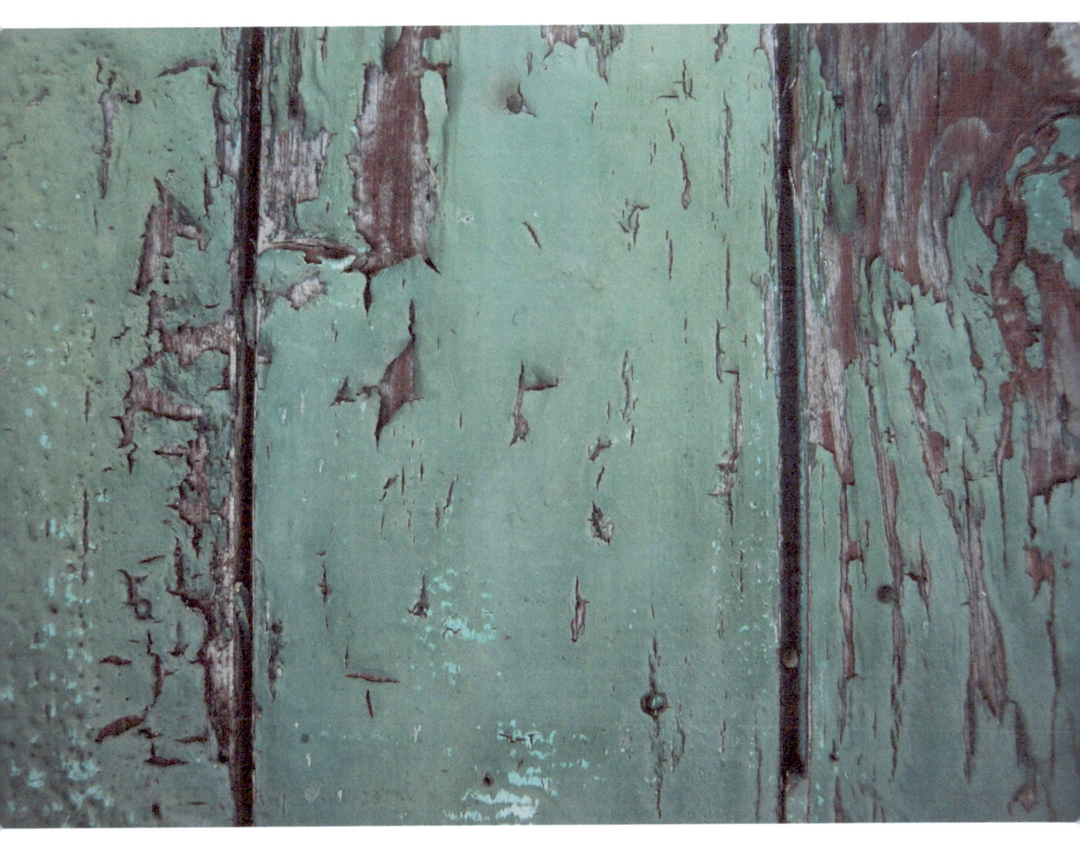

The pleasure of abiding. The pleasure of insistence, of persistence. The pleasure of obligation, the pleasure of dependency. The pleasures of ordinary devotion. The pleasure of recognizing that one may have to undergo the same realizations, write the same notes in the margin, return to the same themes in one's work, relearn the same emotional truths, write the same book over and over again – not because one is stupid or obstinate or incapable of change, but because such revisitations constitute a life.

/ Maggie Nelson

That is, my difference is very particular, but no more particular than anyone's, touchingly. You know, it turns out candor can also be a practice of displacing one's self-centrality.

/ Brian Blanchfield

If they ask you, tell them we were flying.

/ Stefano Harney & Fred Moten

two/

A BEGINNING /

Leaving everything behind
    and being left behind
    started me.
    That, and poverty.
The things we didn't have
    or couldn't do.
The language she didn't speak,
    the shoes I couldn't wear.
Absence, always
    absent father
    the too-soon absent brother
    money absence
    a mother choosing absence.
And me, adrift
    absencing from myself
    altering. often.
    my growing mind muddied water.

MOTHERWIT /

my mother never owned a pair of jeans
denim was not in her repertoire
neither was english
but she knew how to count her pennies

SHE /

My favorite sound in the English language is *she*

UNI, OR EVERY DAY THE END OF SOMETHING /

Fatherless,
some with cruel mothers.
Hints of violence
seeping through the concrete slabs
and off-gassing from the carpet.
Privation inside/out.
Exhausted,
spent before spawning.

Baby sea urchins,
unruly black spines flexible,
tumbling with the tide.
Uni on the verge.
Always hungry, and self-satiated.
Careful not to crack in the pounding surf,
be slurped up & out
with a squeeze of unwanted attention
or acidic neglect.
    No matter, *our eyes fill with a wet history.*

It's not my mother's cooking or her concern
that patch me up after being sullied out there.
I steal back my body.
Catharsis with the homies
    in the speak only we can decipher,
    the waves of laughter that have no end.
Collective bliss with abandon.
I've dissolved into our good time.
What we didn't know to call love,
to name nurture.

Transcendence of a kind,
those school days spent in our section 8 apartments,
Havens, in a current with another rhythm.
A familiar defiance between us,
and a *mutual melancholy.*
Uplift in sneaking loosies bought with stolen change,
in the patties you fired up and put on that airy bread.
13, working your deep fryer like a boss,
having learned how to take good care
after your moms left
to somewhere in Ohio
neither of us had ever been.

It was years of leaving myself,
drifting my way to something, anything,
different, better, beautiful.
My departure *anticipated and implied,*
from one school to the next to the next to the next,
So I could return a visitor to those homes that raised us.
But *the structures we inhabit, inhabit us*
and still, my return *ongoing.*

THE BLOCK /

The terrace the block my block.
Up the block, down the block.
Building my building the stairs.
1st floor 2nd floor 3rd.
Upstairs downstairs.
Ring the bell, buzz me in.
18th street 19th street 20th street, my street.
Across the street.
The benches the basement the office the train
the roof the river the hill the gate.
The fire escape.

MAKERS /

The people I come from,
they're known for their epic poems.

But my Ithaka is Queens.
And if I met seducing sirens on my way,
they have me with anything consciousness-bending.

And I know that the drink isn't a homecoming,
That I can have access to these parts without the twist.

But here I am, again.
Liquid medicine.
Liquid rarified to ether. To spirit.
Liquid transmissions.

I am your vessel twisted clear,
vessel in pulsating joy, in prayer with tears.
The blood-thump beat.
The hips flexed in rhythm.
The deep need to soften,
all that embodied sorrow.

Grief, alright. But not for too long.
Not for this many years.
Not into adulthood. Not after motherhood.
Not grief with consequences.

My challenges, adolescent.
My inheritance, first generation.
I who exceed and by exceeding escape
It is in making that I make my way out.

For Ammones, Who Died Aged 29, In 610

Raphael, they want you to compose a few verses
as an epitaph for the poet Ammones.
Something polished and in good taste. You
can do it, you are the appropriate person to write
as befits the poet Ammones, our very own.

You must, of course, mention his poems-
but you should also speak about his beauty,
his delicate beauty that we loved.

Your Greek has always been elegant and musical.
But we're in need of your entire skill now.
Our love and our sorrow pass into a foreign tongue.
Pour your Egyptian feeling into the foreign tongue.

Raphael, your verses must be written in such a way
that they contain, you know, something in them of our lives,
that both cadence as well as every phrase denote,
that an Alexandrian is writing about an Alexandrian.

/ C.P. Cavafy

I survived all the deaths
the evaded end of my birth
the death of a girl in her home/land
the death of being a father's daughter.
The poverty, the humiliations, the neglect, the betrayals
    / all of it death-scented.
The coca-fueled short circuits.
The dawns of near-death, prayer-escaped death
    / I wasn't found dead in my room at 29, it wasn't me.

Ghosts in sunlight may very well find rest
But some things you don't unknow.
    Now free and not incarcerated.
    Now heart beating and not dead.
    Now walking out and not caught.
    Now in possession and not found out.
I got away with it.
Not with agency, with white fortune.
My mother's seers must have burned
the hex-breaking candles at both ends.
She believed the demitasse,
Coffee grinds parting / an open path to the new world.

But you, the two of you, were brought forth in love and desire,
with resoluteness in the inevitability of your living.
The body, spirit-filled,
little fists propelled into the breeze with abandon.
Tangled hair, sun-kissed skin, buck teeth, wild smiles.
Iconography of minor saints,
traces of mother's milk on you still.
To give, and give and give some more,
care again and again
on and on, 'til you were free.
More free than me /

LOVE LETTER /

The signs, the signs, the no's
and our hijacked yes in the sealed city.
The loud internal yes
that turns our posture and our walk.

We stride, no, soar
and the sidewalk sizzles.
We get lifted the ways we know how,
make use of streetlamps,
phonebooth shelters;
a place to rest our backs and spark up,
watching the threshold between us melt into bliss.

Expanses of asphalt *here, on the edge of everything.*
Claiming public walls,
the everyday praxis of taking space.
Scaling bridges to say *will wuz here*
when you were actually meant to be disappeared.
The outlaw's mark
under cover of night,
leaving a gemtrail to the secret city.
Nothing here to buy, crave, aspire to, measure against.
Just to survive all you've seen - in all its realness.

You're the keepers of my true wild.
Undead kings,
your molten insignia waxed on my every move.
You raised me like second mothers.
    I did the same for you.
My humanity sharpened on your crests
so that we're chill evermore.

There's a stillness to this place,
an unexpected quiet.
The apartment buildings
stark and jagged – just how I like my graffiti.
This is where we work it out.
From ever-expulsion to selfhood,
experimented on the curb, against the fence.
In abandoned nighttime places,
we teach one another about inner authority,
wondering how we know what we do,
this easy intellectuality and wit.
The word conspire means breathe together, comrades,
and we do
into one another's interiority
doing the energy work
of making meaning through mood.

Two roofs between us
from where we could see the skyline and the chasm.
If I turned to the moon
you would be there,
skin catching the flood lights off the building.
Yourself incandescent, refracting.
In our classrooms, in the courtyard, at home -
more important what others said about us
not what we said about ourselves.
But on the roof
it's our desire and d e l i g h t,
where we can tend to one another softly, in privacy,
slip into one another in the *black balm of late night,*
while watching the hood from above.
Remembering together what has not yet been,
crafting ourselves and our freedom.

WITH AND FOR /

A band of goats with no shepherd,
nimble-footed through the streets.
Show up to the park
looking for, or with,
spirit-party things.
A park with an ethos,
with everything to say about current, flow, cruise.
And we did our best to listen
to the *outcast mass intellectuality of the fringe,*
galvanizing the think that would endure and matter
perched around the fountain.

Inheritors of the bohemian quarters
of this city of cities,
worlds beyond the block.
Kid emissaries of promise and possibility,
of a dailiness lushly lived.
I remake my place in the world, in your company.
I'm all intuition and mounting resistance
    that was *before the long discipline*
    of making sense of what one has seen.
My future is in this present free fall
and there's a settling of my true nature
in the variety of dissent, and style, in my midst.
All these seekers answering the call to disruption,
on the way to another place altogether,
a radiant transfiguration ongoing / unfolding / already.

Needing to rest,
spent from our minor uprisings and experimentations,
the *noise of objection* receding
to the refuge of your room.

There's an optimism to our breathless ascent
to the 6th floor walkup.
While strawberry mom's at work
we've occupied her rent controlled gem,
an incubator for the practice of intimacy and fellowship.

A self-directed space teeming with decadence and autonomy.
Matchbook-sized small.
Room enough for the whole flock
on the mattress,
sheets worn soft.

The spectacle of us, limbs spilling onto the floor.
Overhead, a canopy of webbed ephemera,
Tangled, hanging from the ceiling.
And us, unafraid to be together,
boundaries between us disappeared,
friend-drunk.

Hand drawn map of the untamed street grid,
your corner of the city sharpied on the wall.
We'll make use of that later,
linked arms stomping our way to the subway,
    an everyday choreography of the possible.

For now,
psychic flights in unison
to the wild beyond
that's on the inside.
Unlikely wonderworkers,
I write the hagiography of the undercommons,
of our friendships, and their project,
in remembrance of how the outside became the worthiest of my regard.

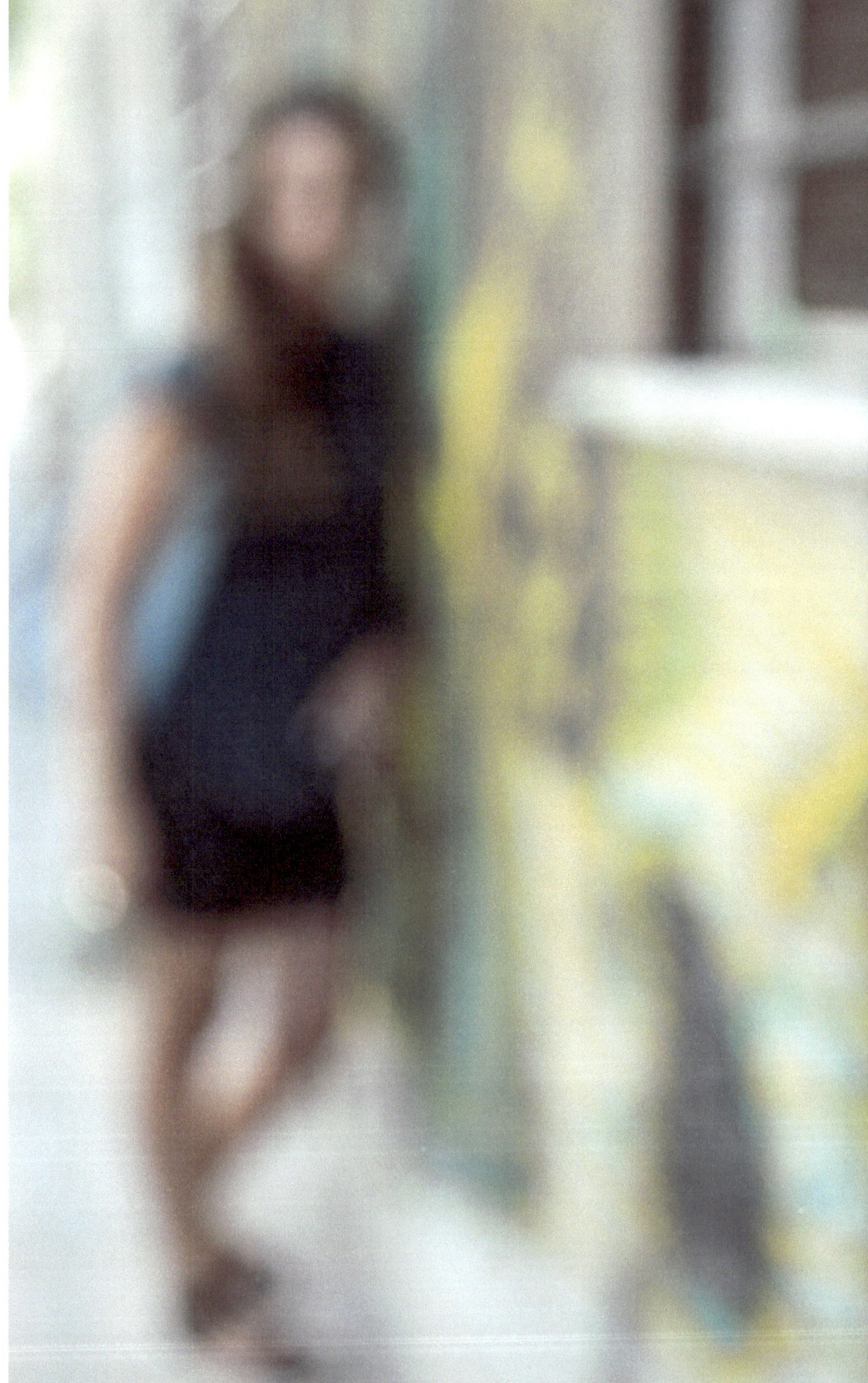

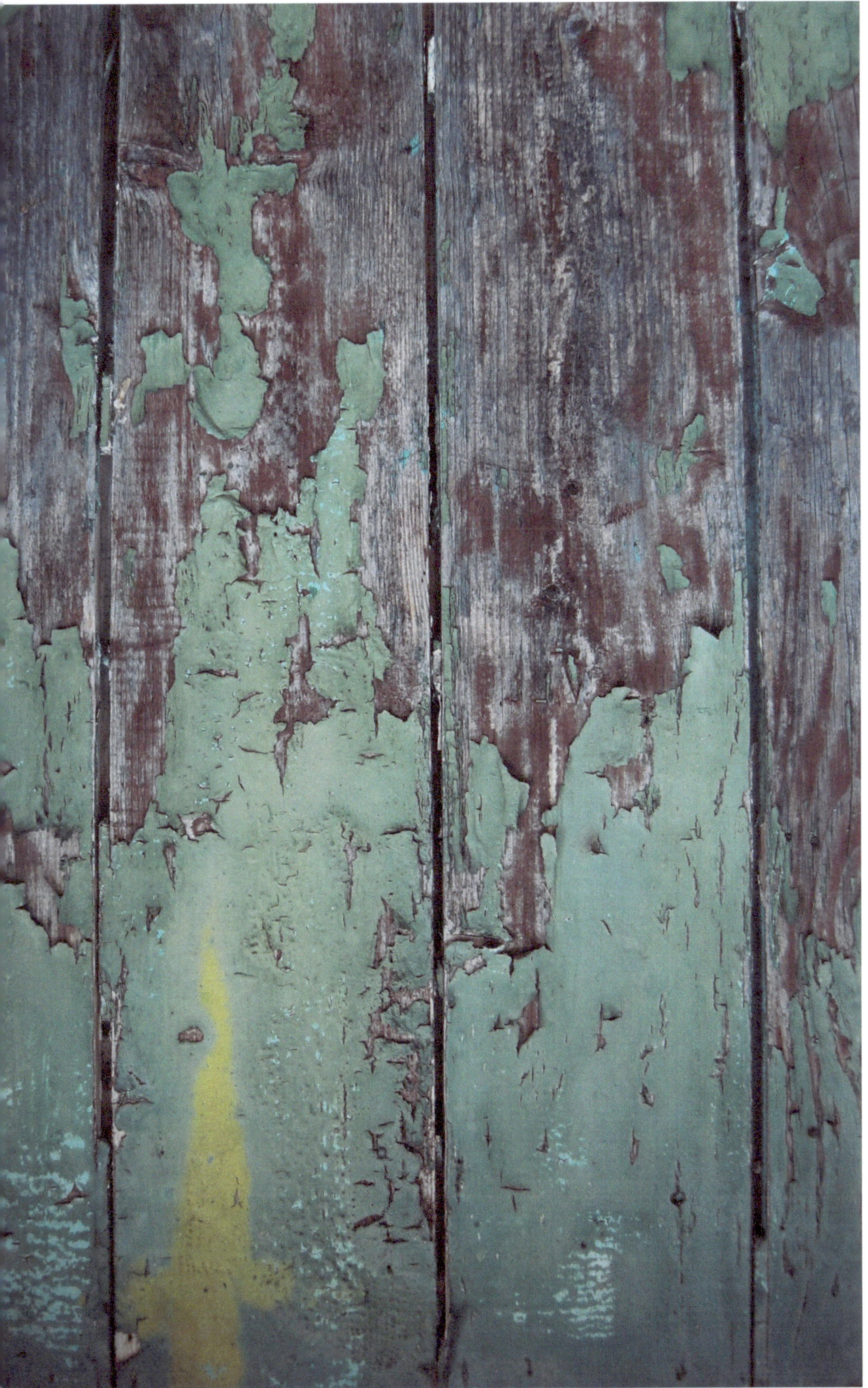

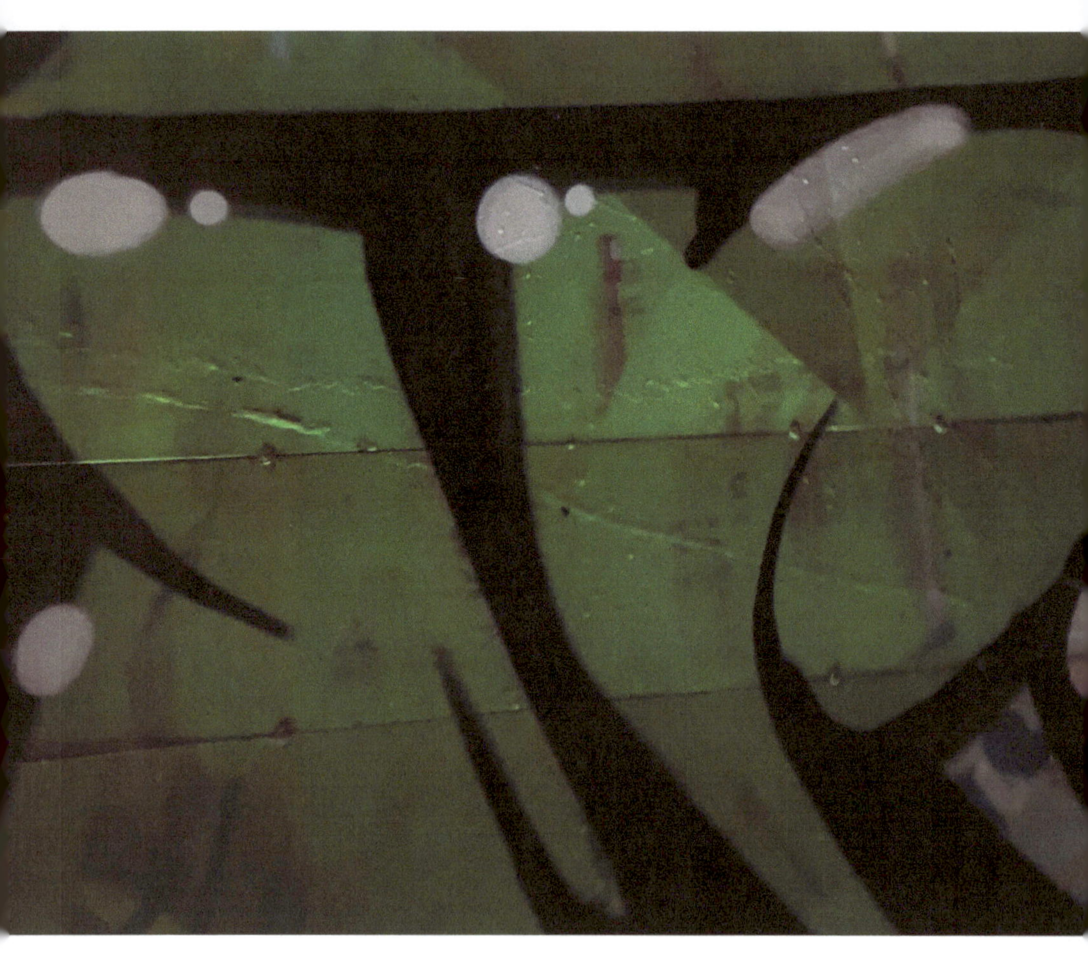

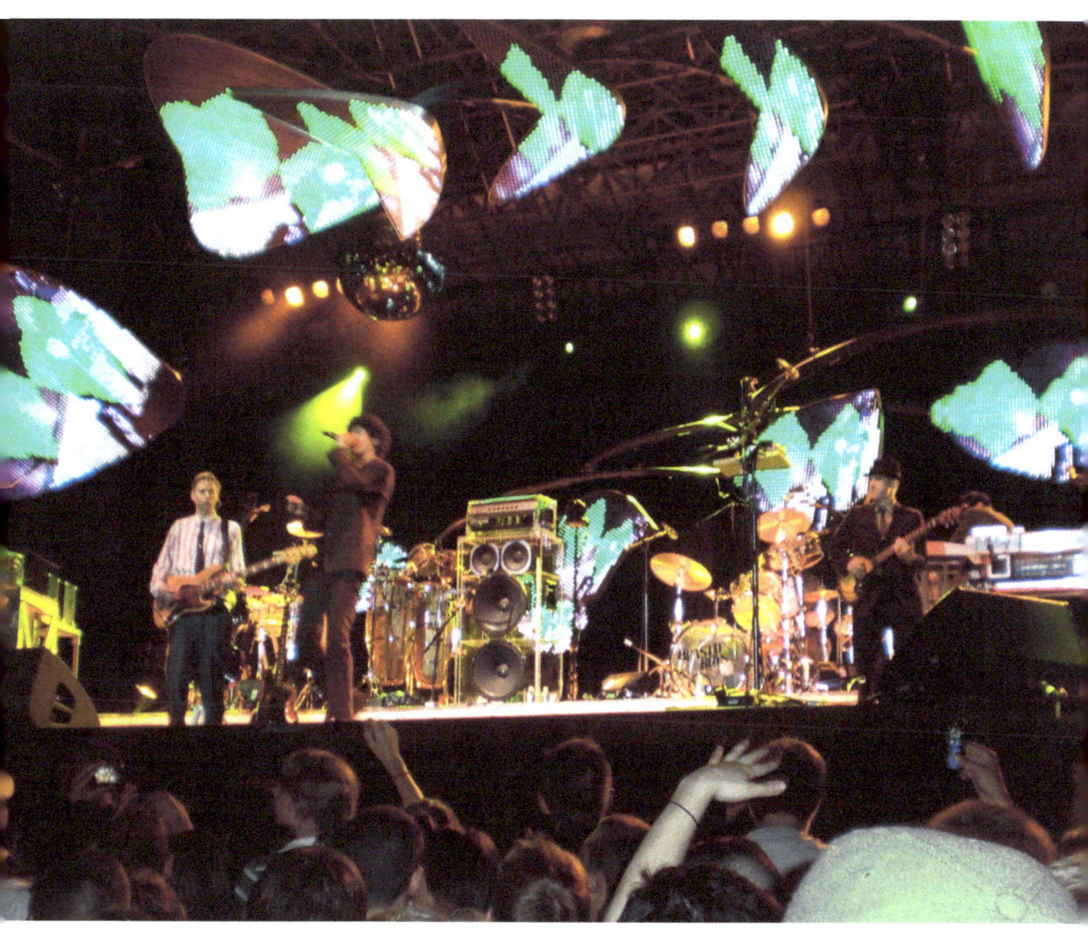

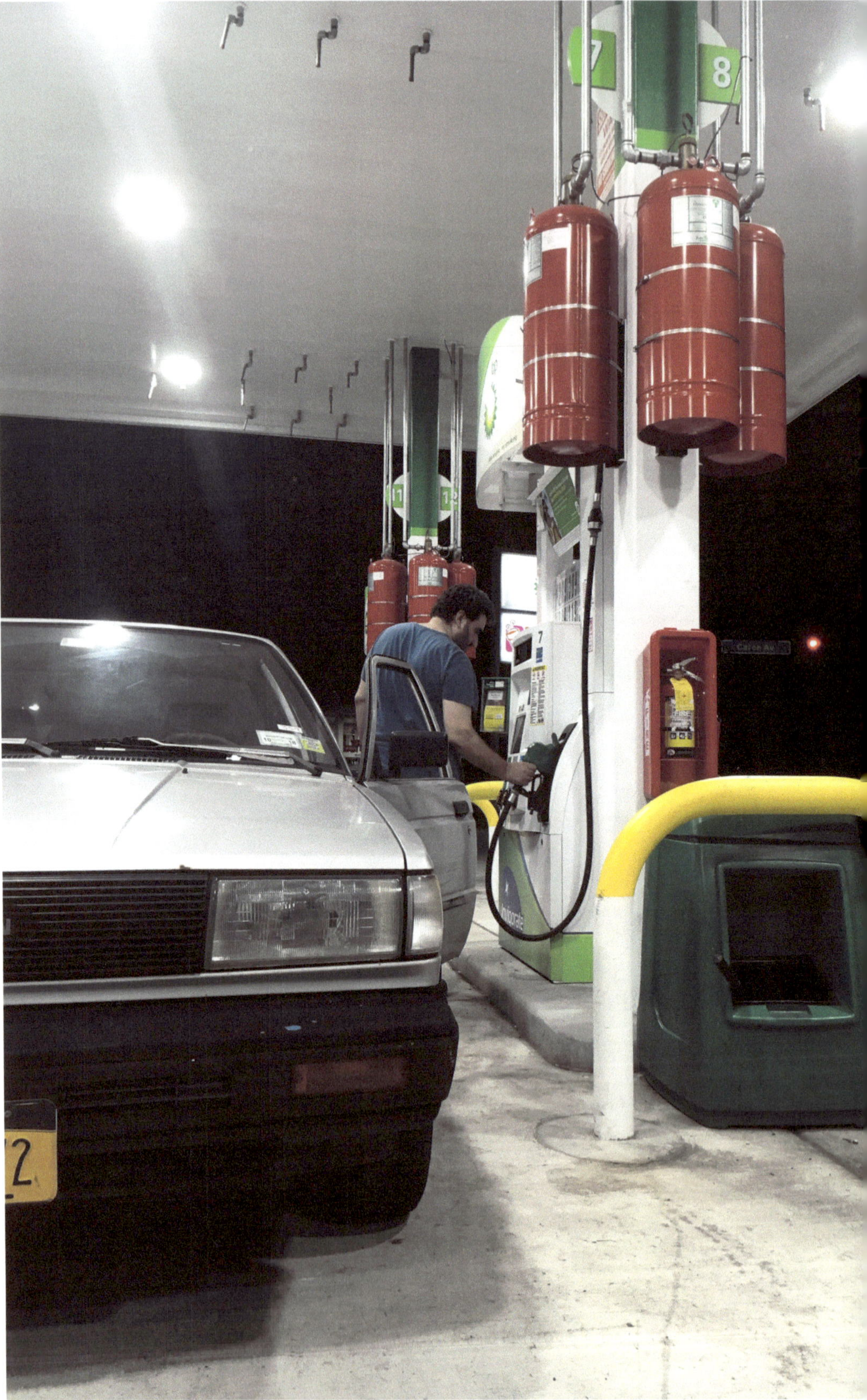
7
8

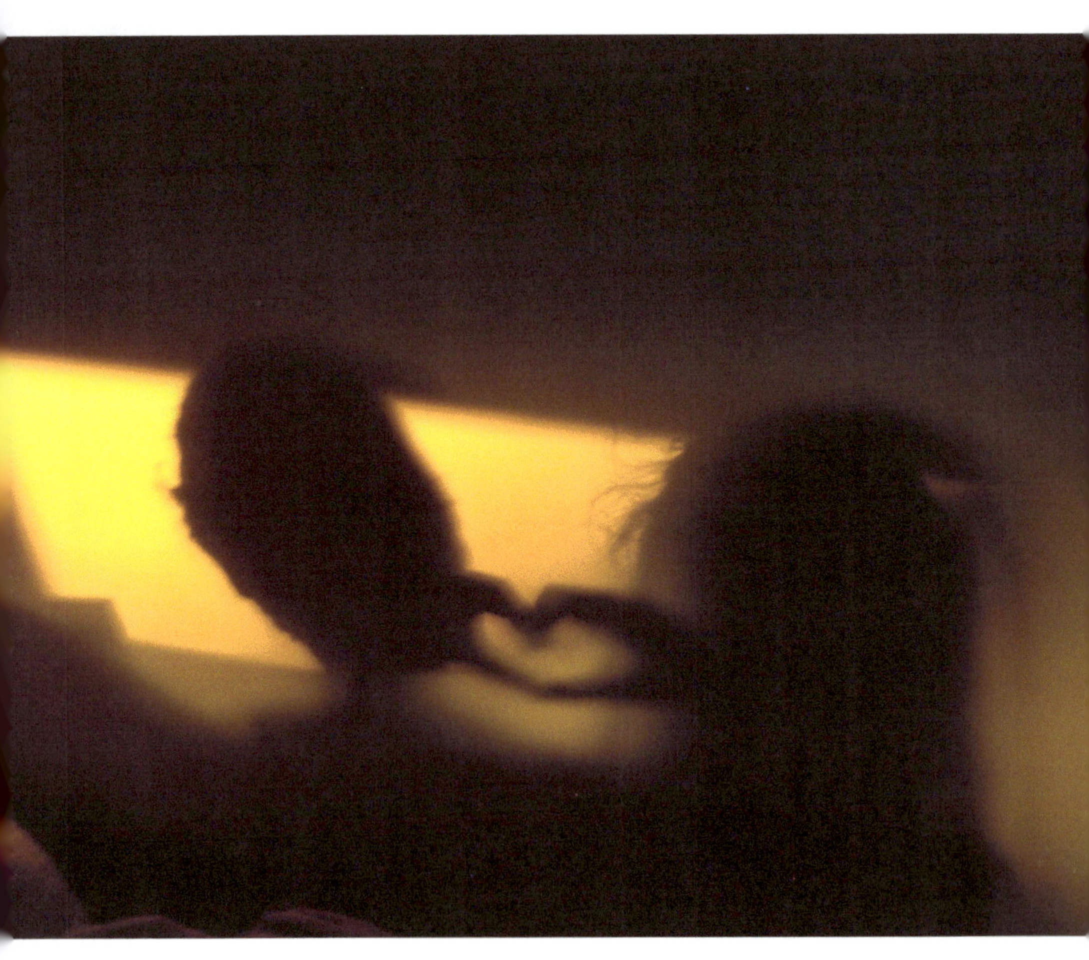

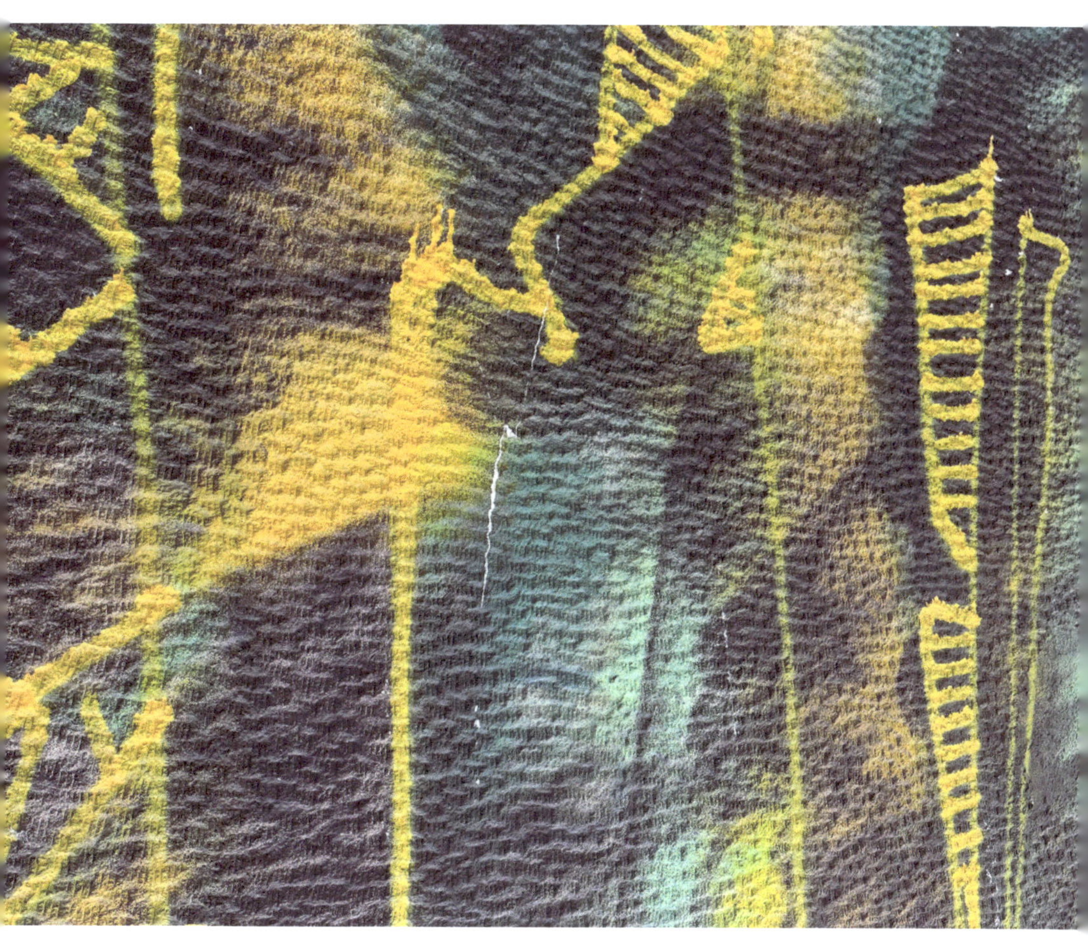

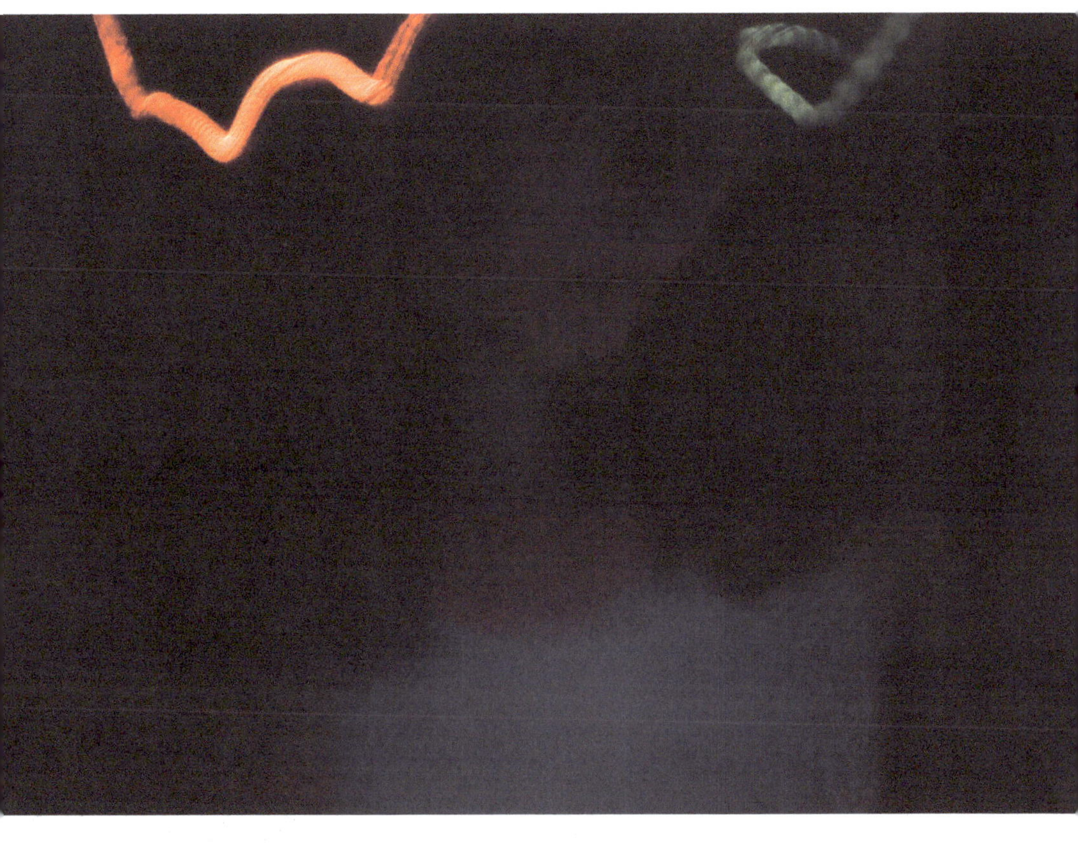

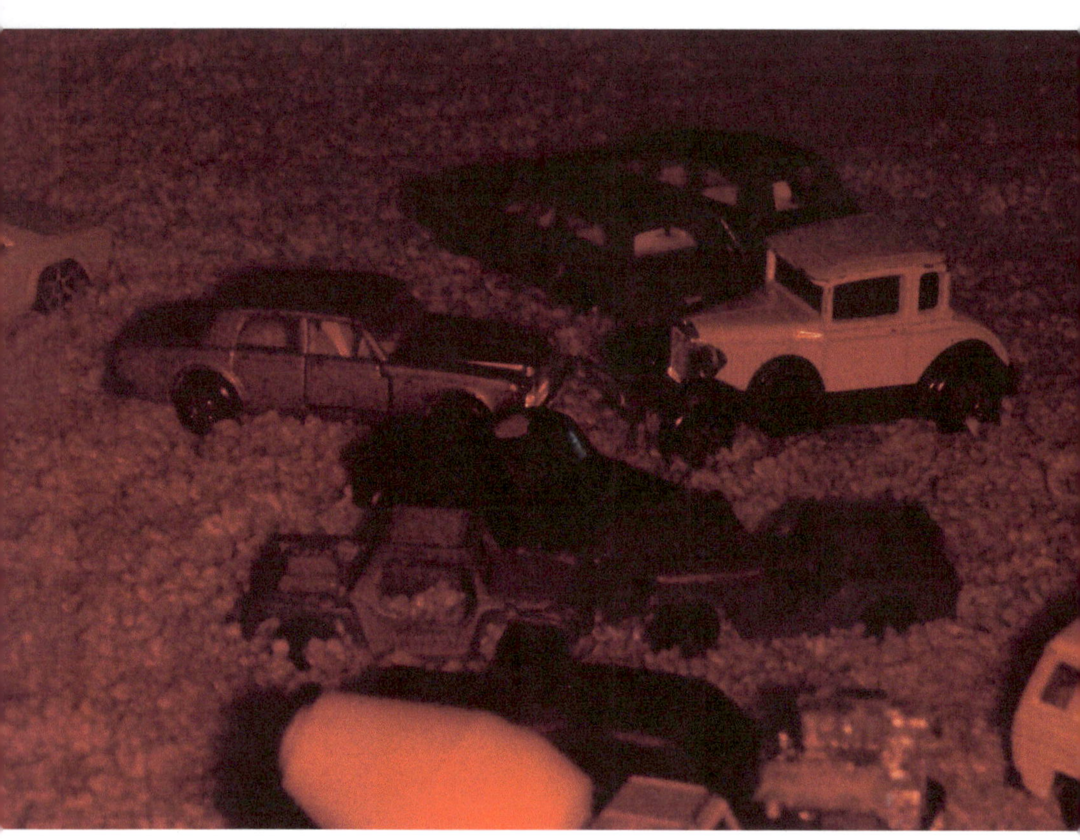

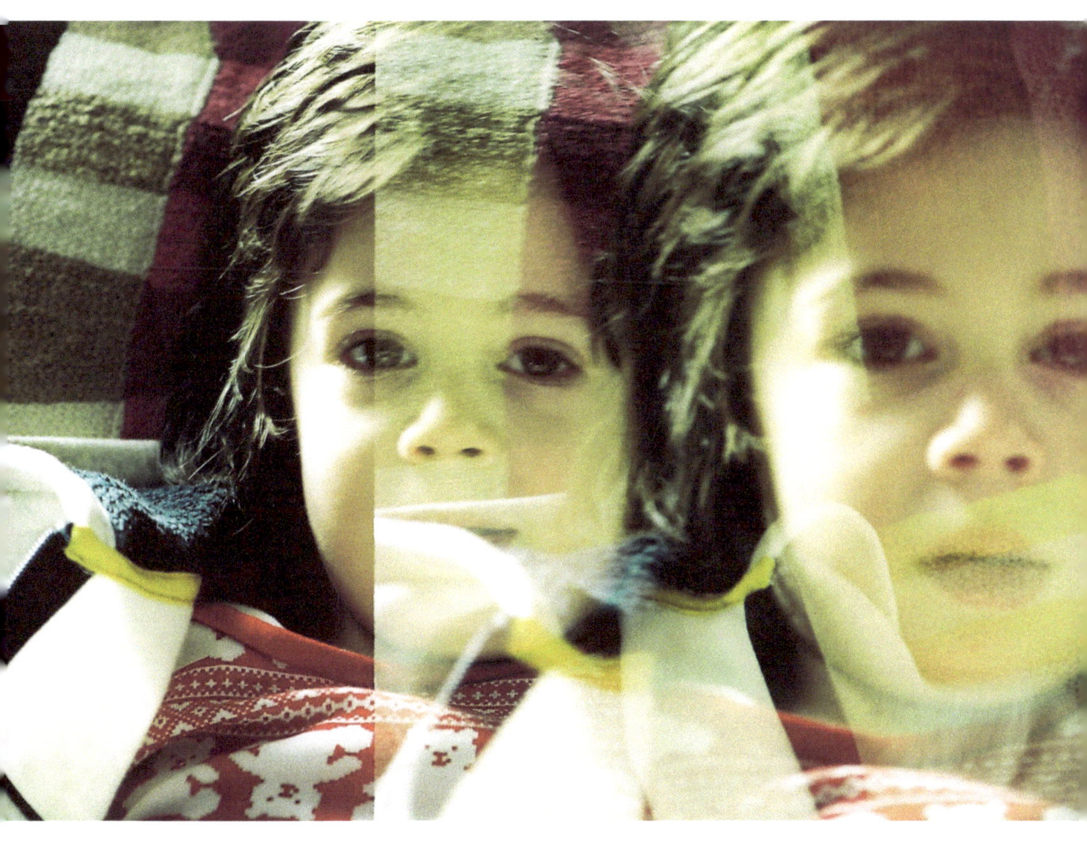

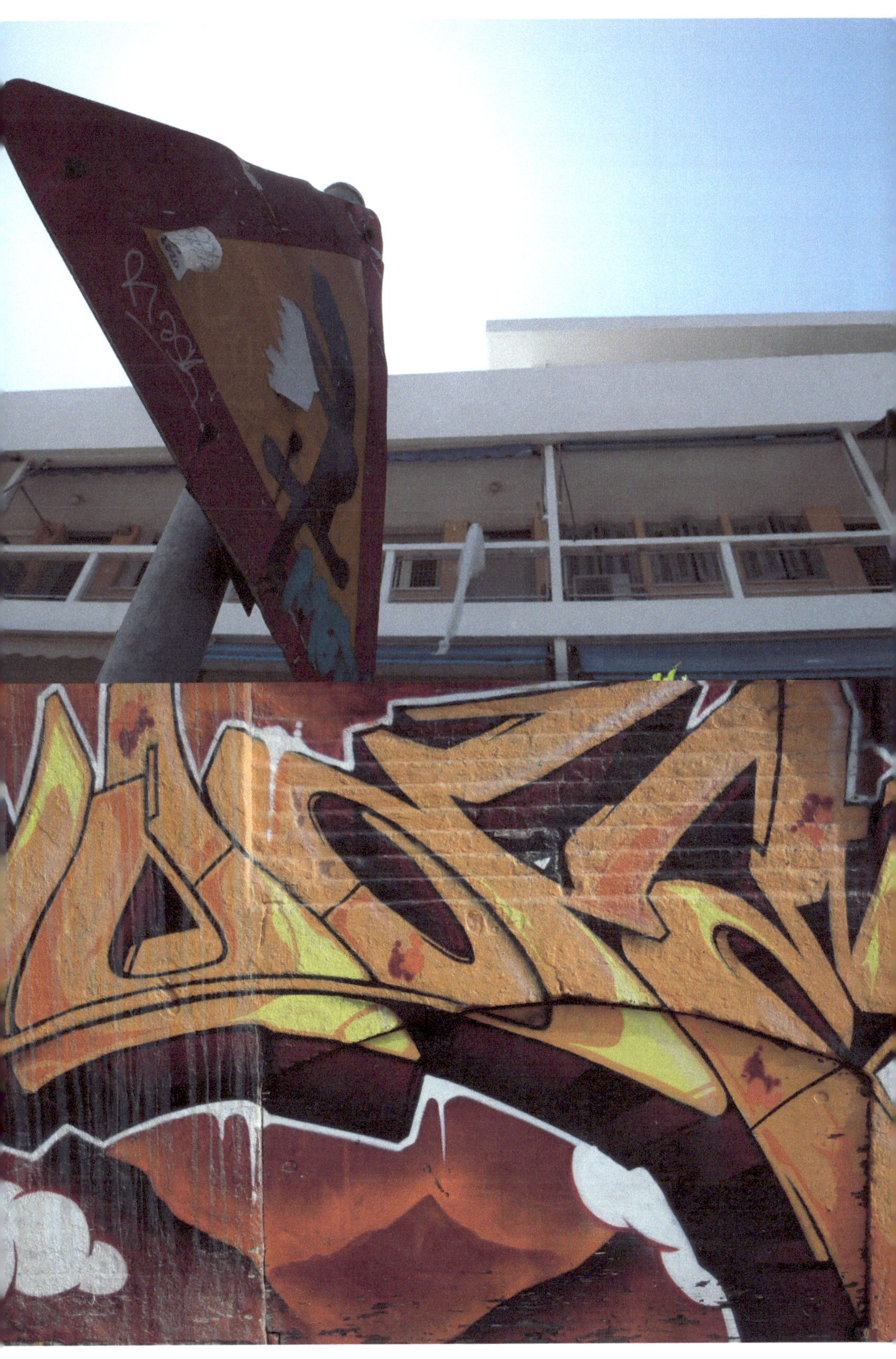

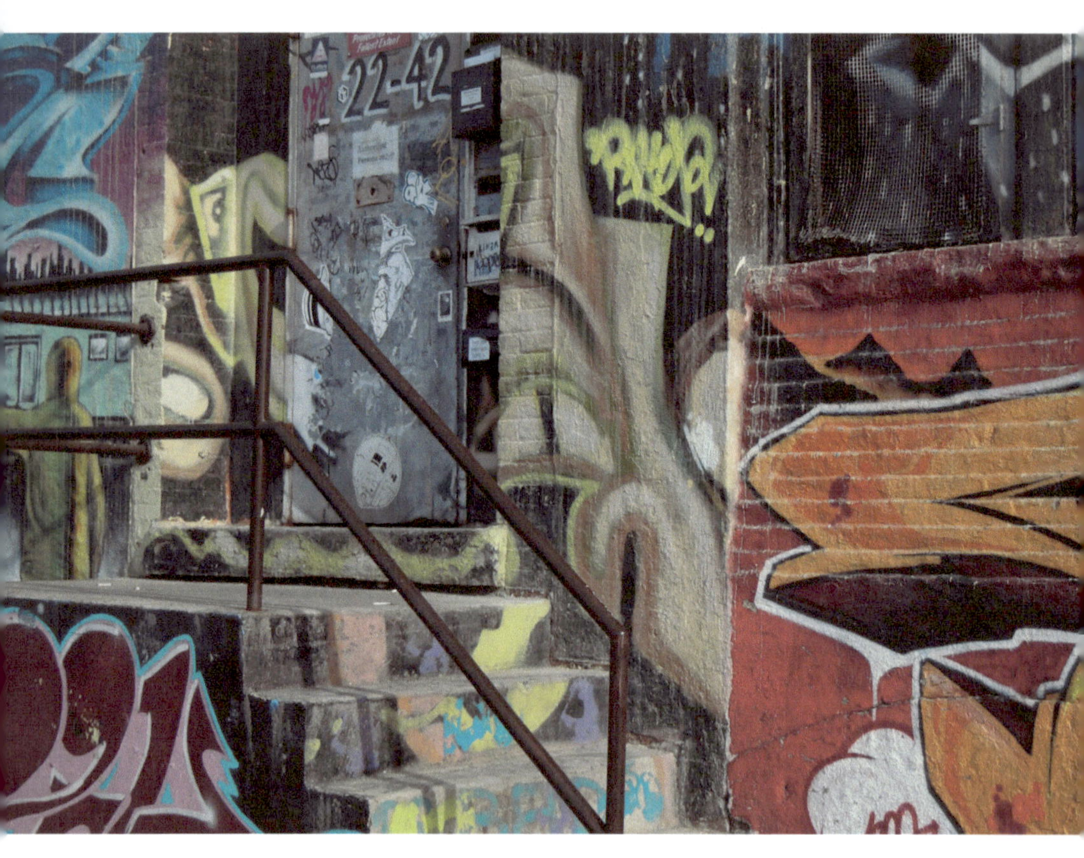
22-42

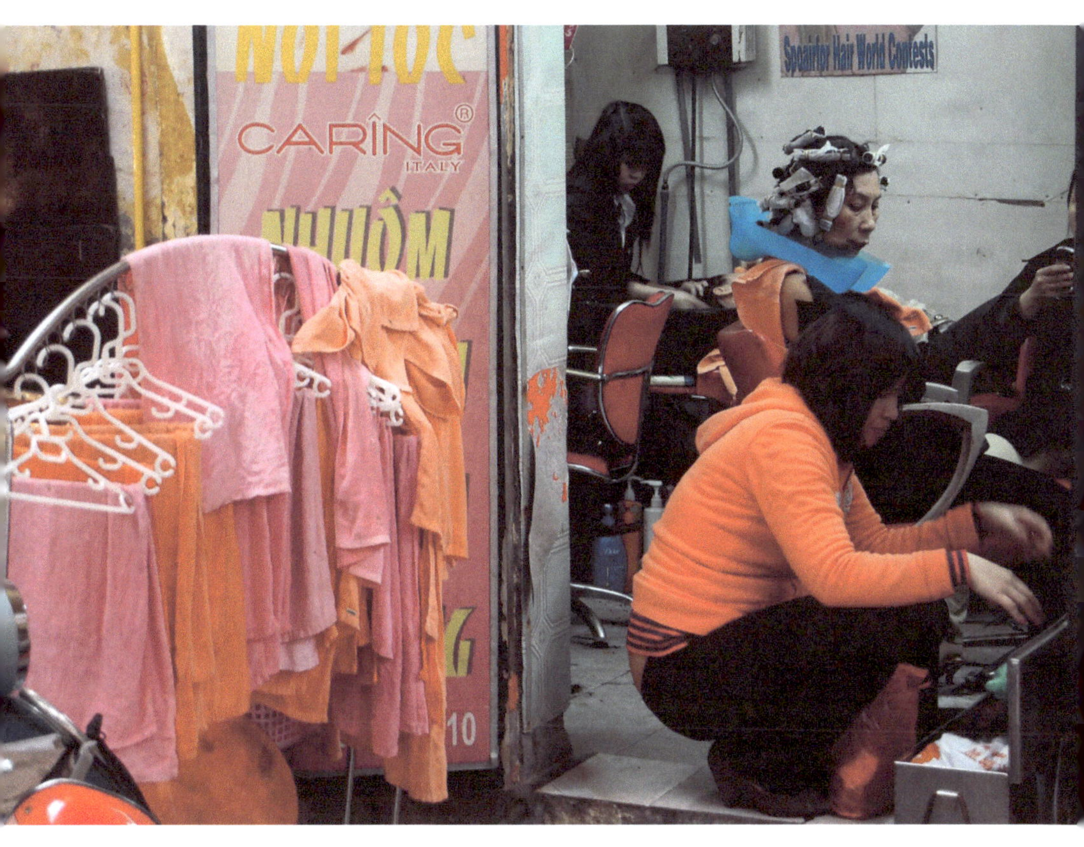
CARÎNG®
ITALY
Hair World Contests

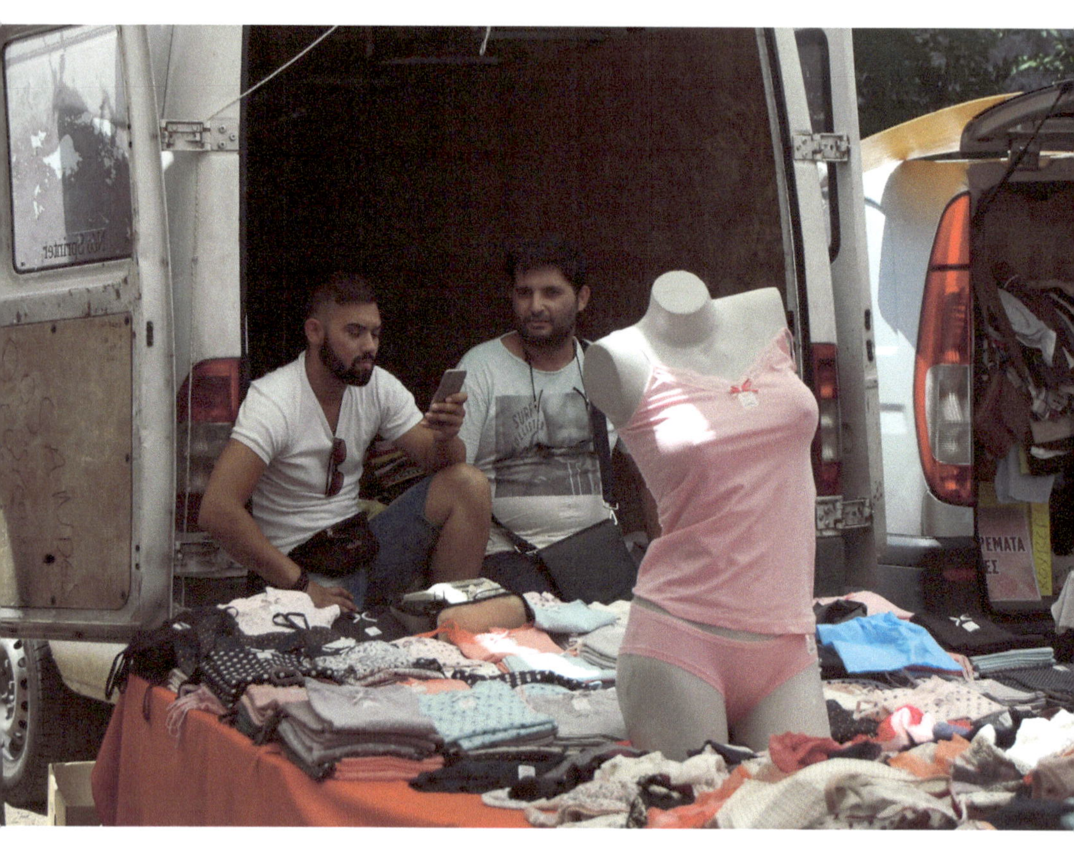

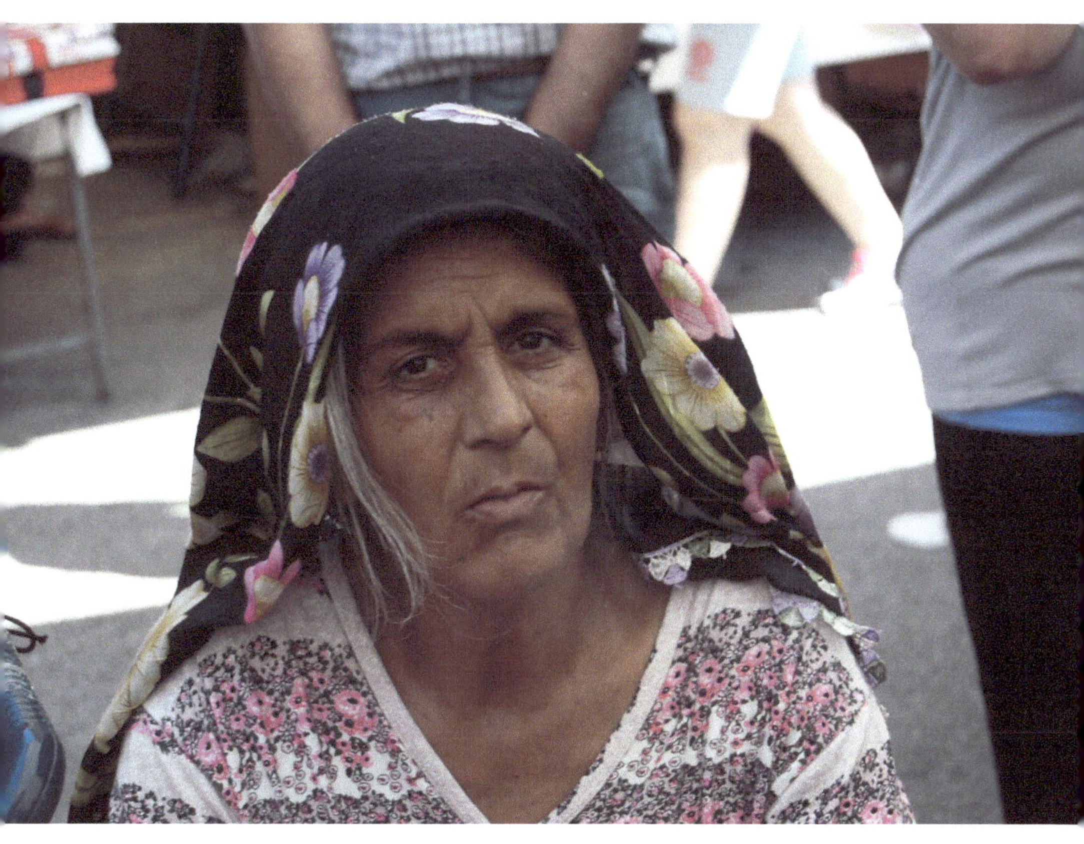

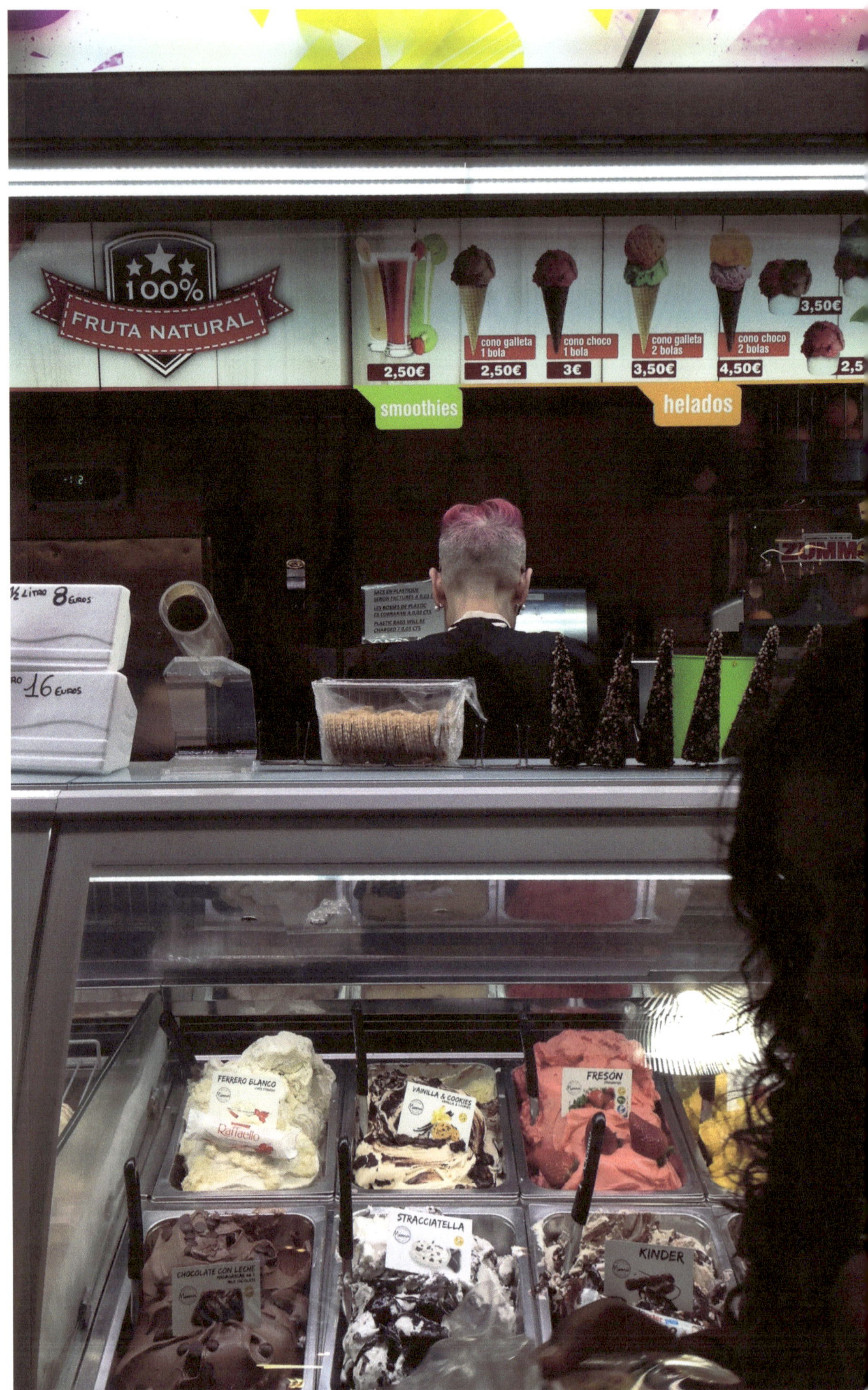
100%
FRUTA NATURAL
2,50€
cono galleta
1 bola
2,50€
cono choco
1 bola
3€
cono galleta
2 bolas
3,50€
cono choco
2 bolas
4,50€
3,50€
smoothies
helados
½ Litro 8 Euros
16 Euros
FERRERO BLANCO
Raffaello
VAINILLA & COOKIES
FRESÓN
STRACCIATELLA
CHOCOLATE CON LECHE
KINDER

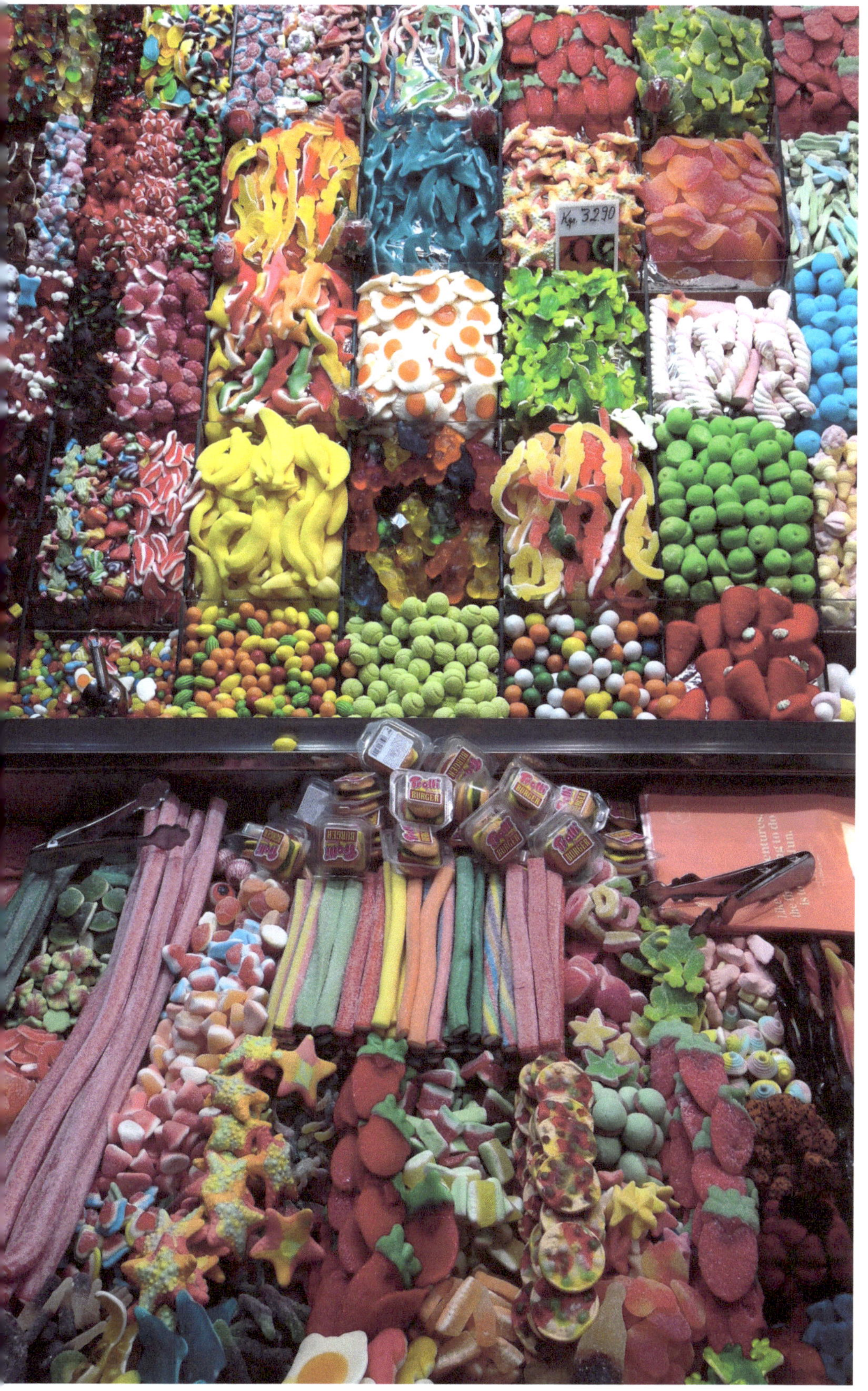
Kgr. 32.90
Trolli
BURGER

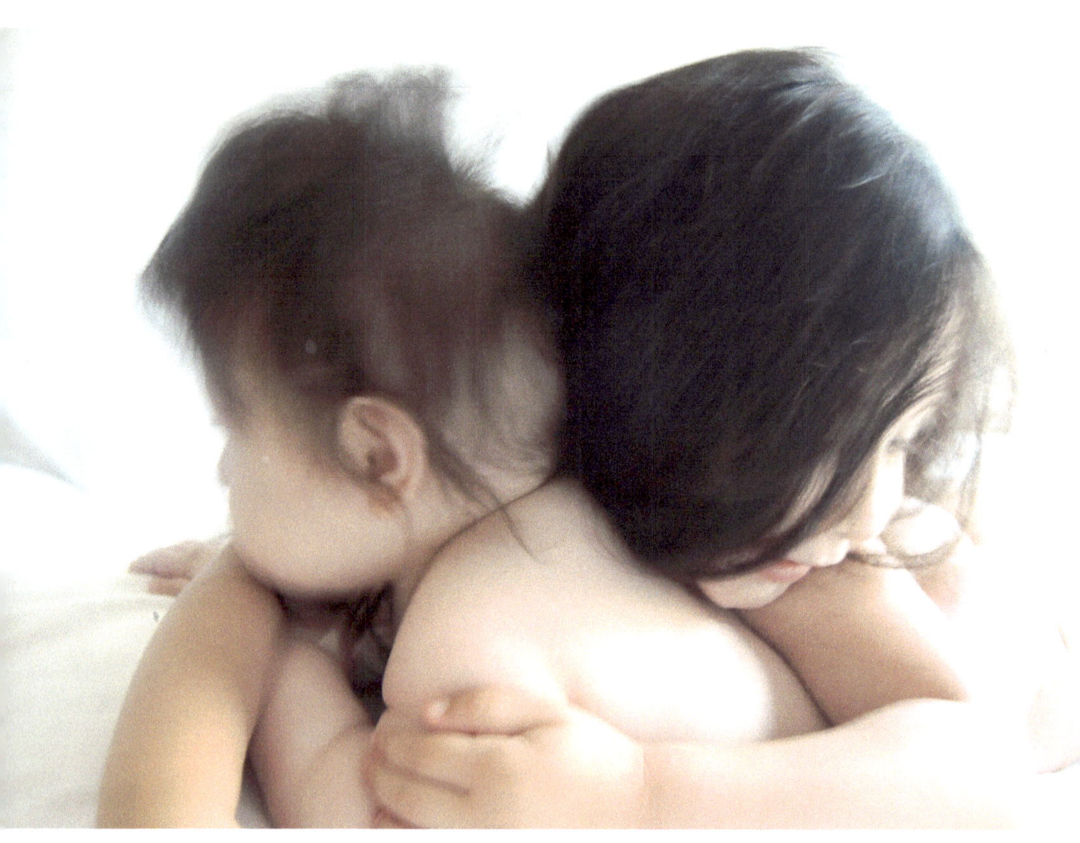

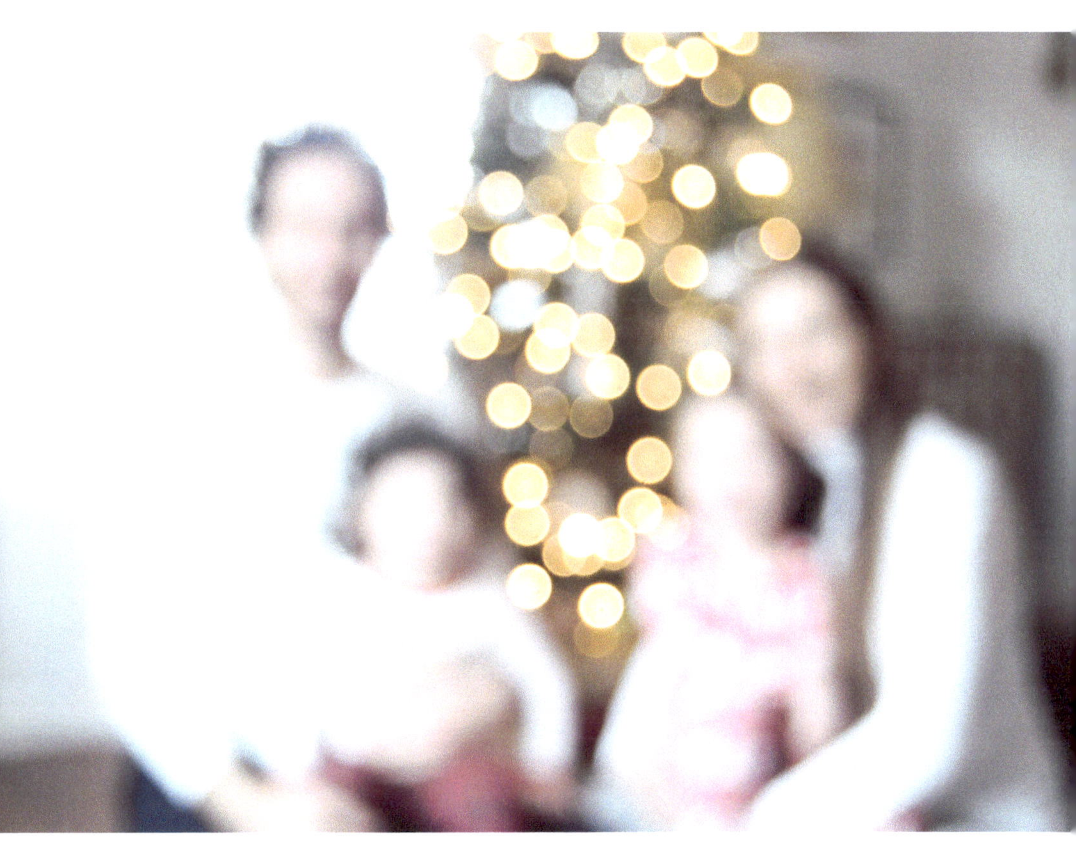

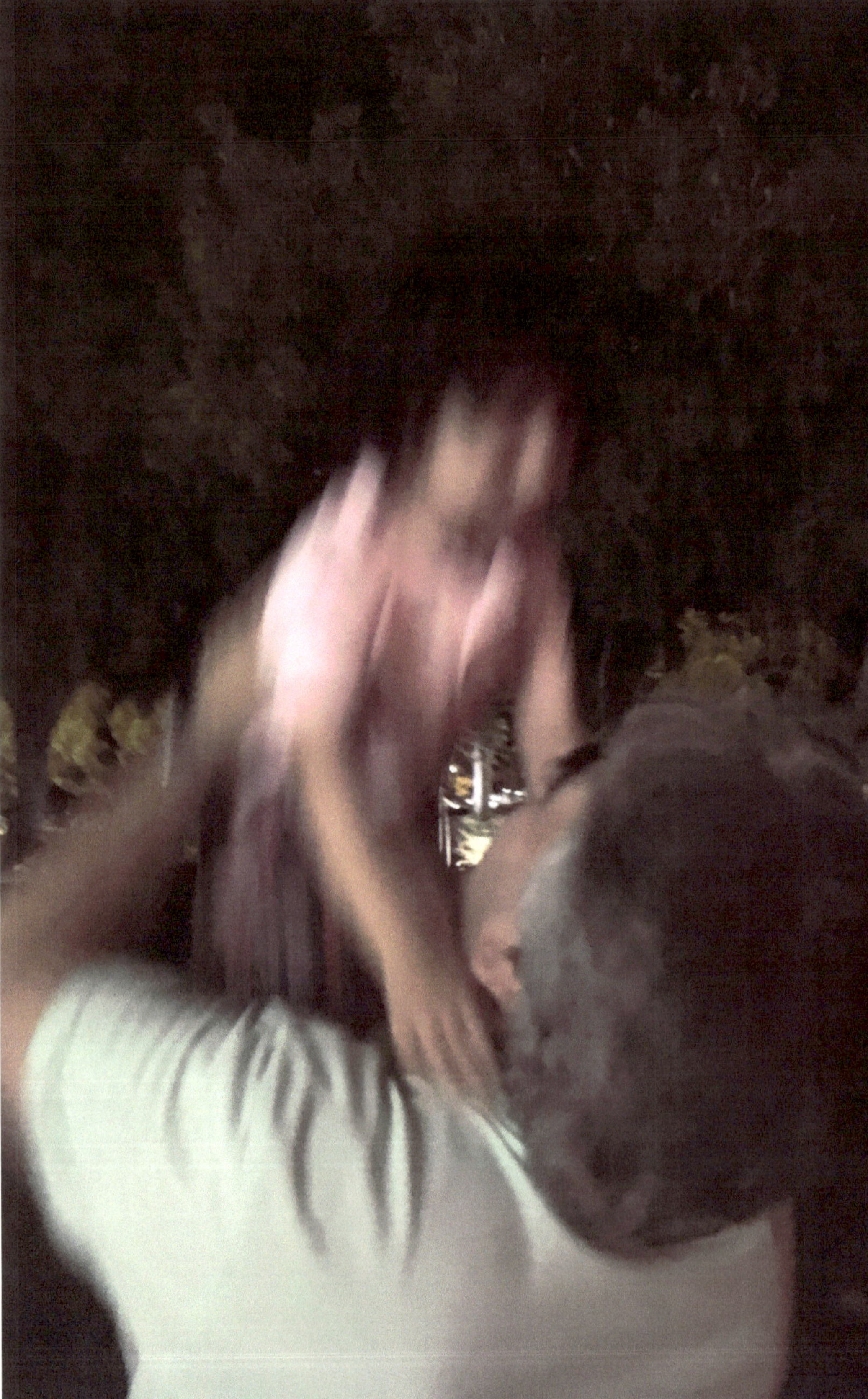

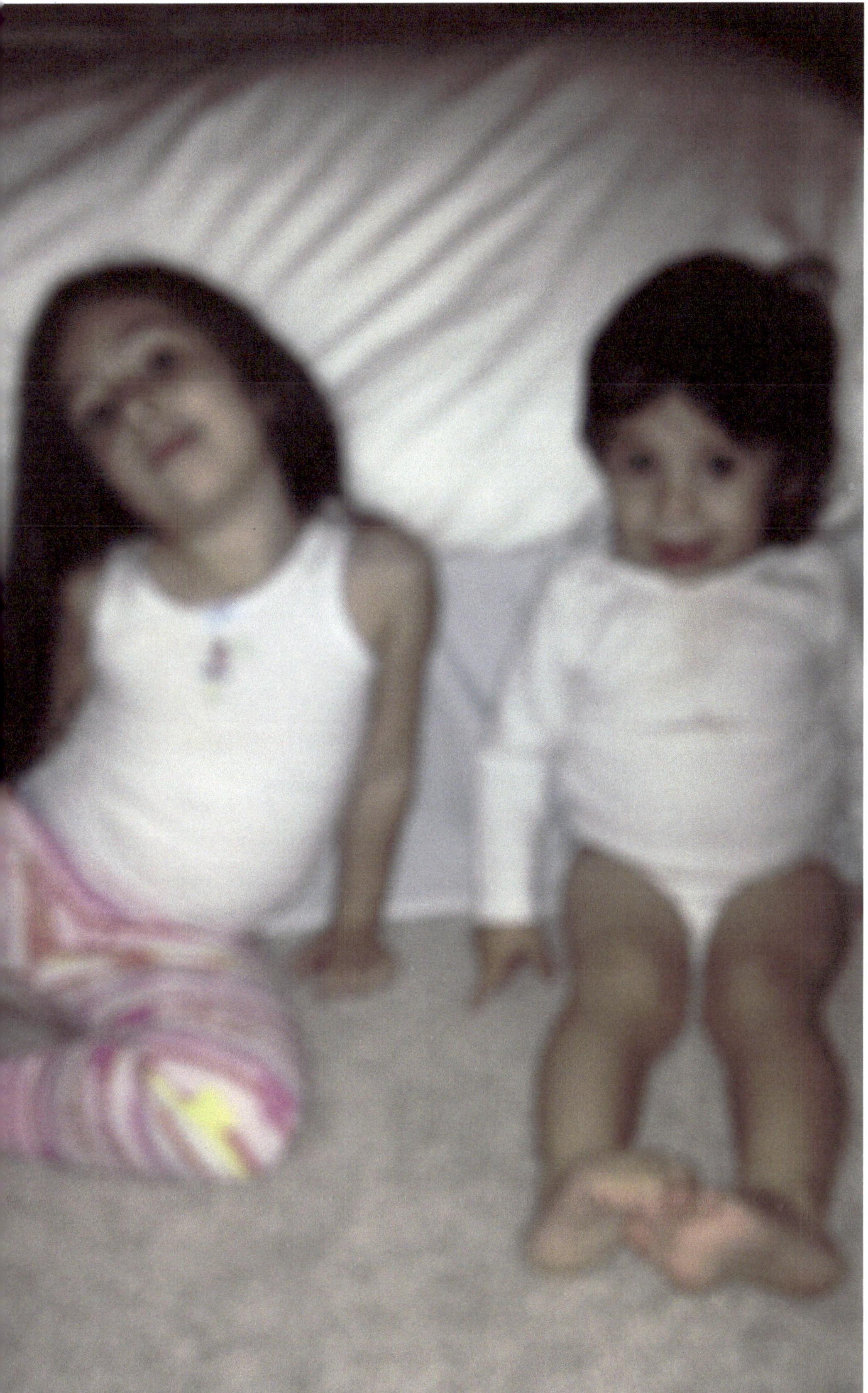

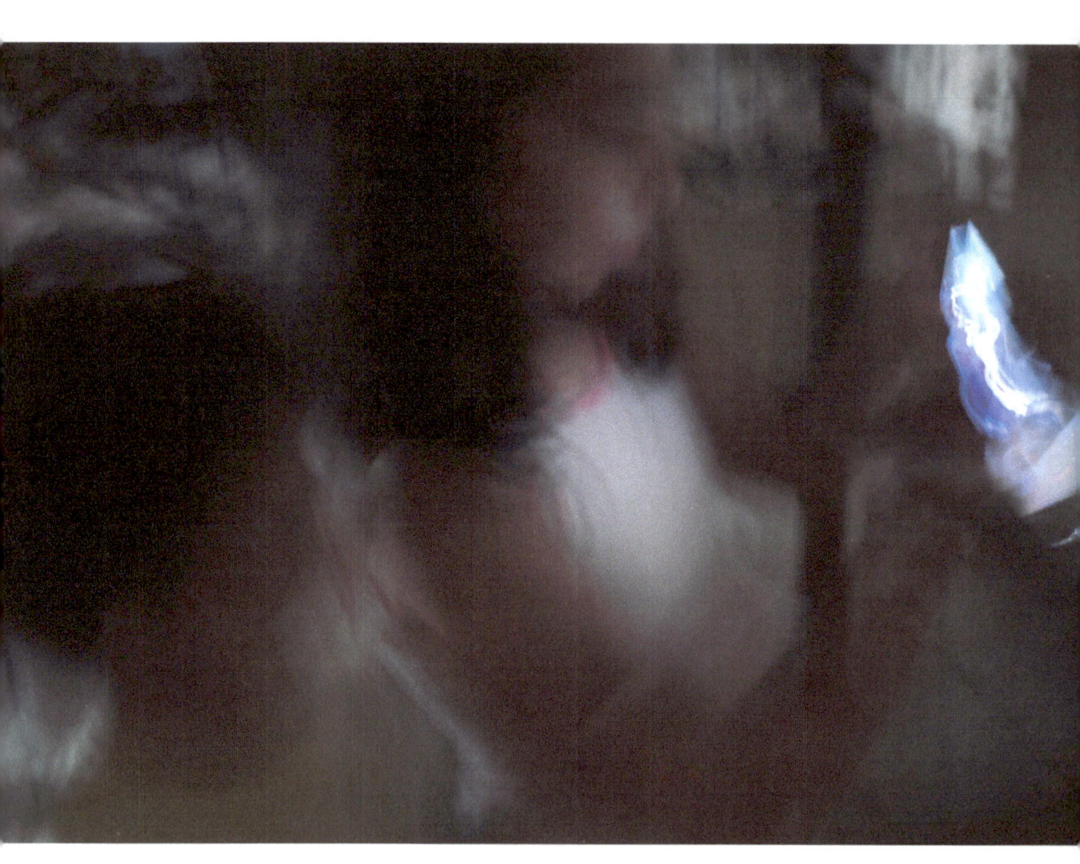

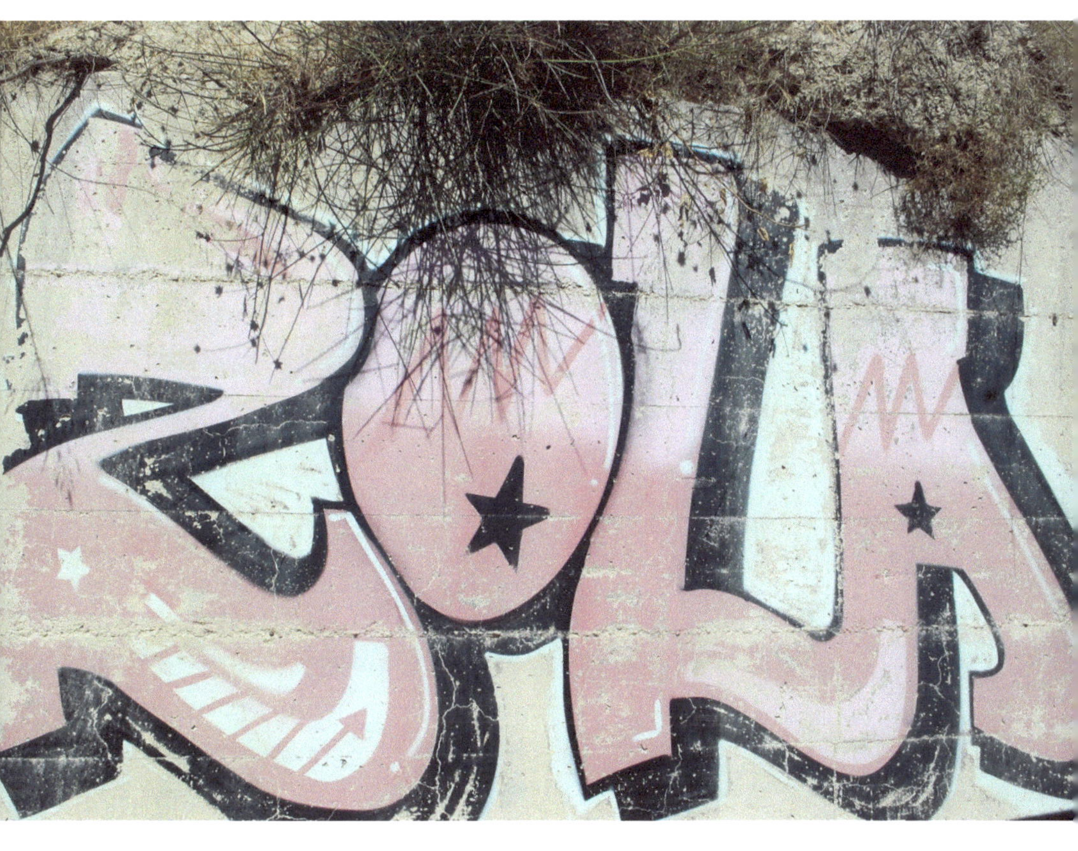

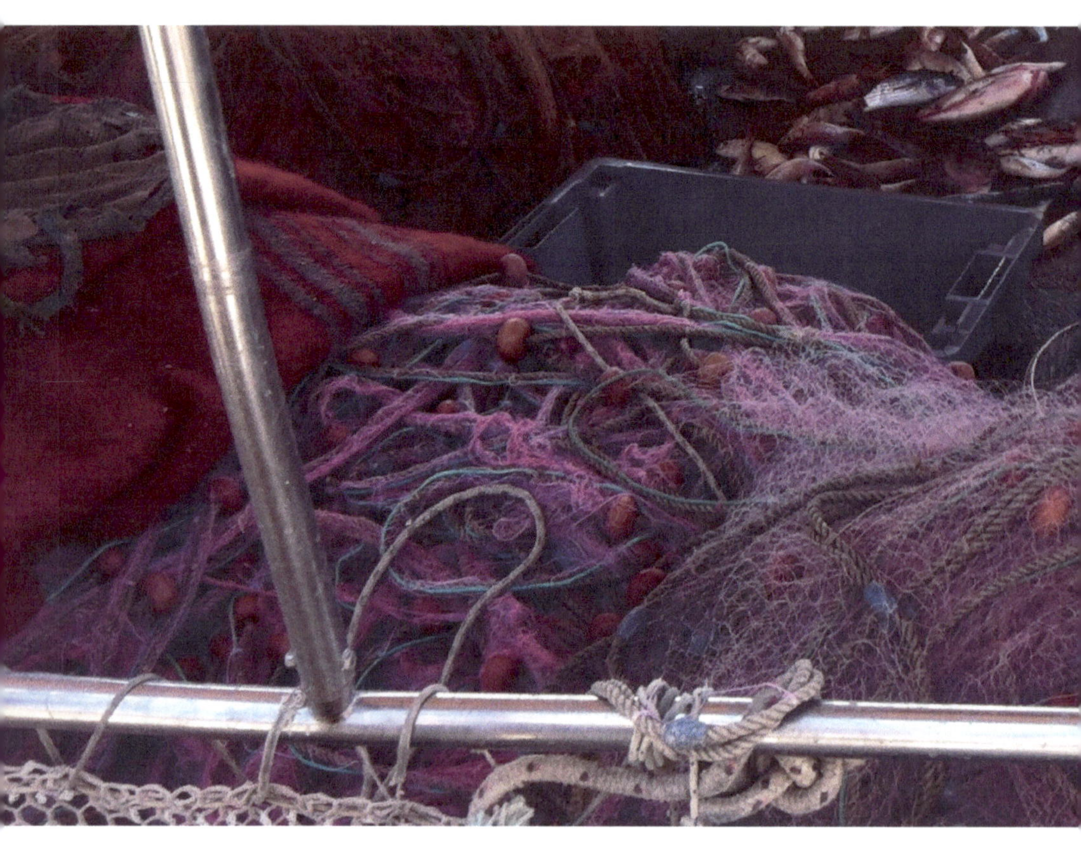

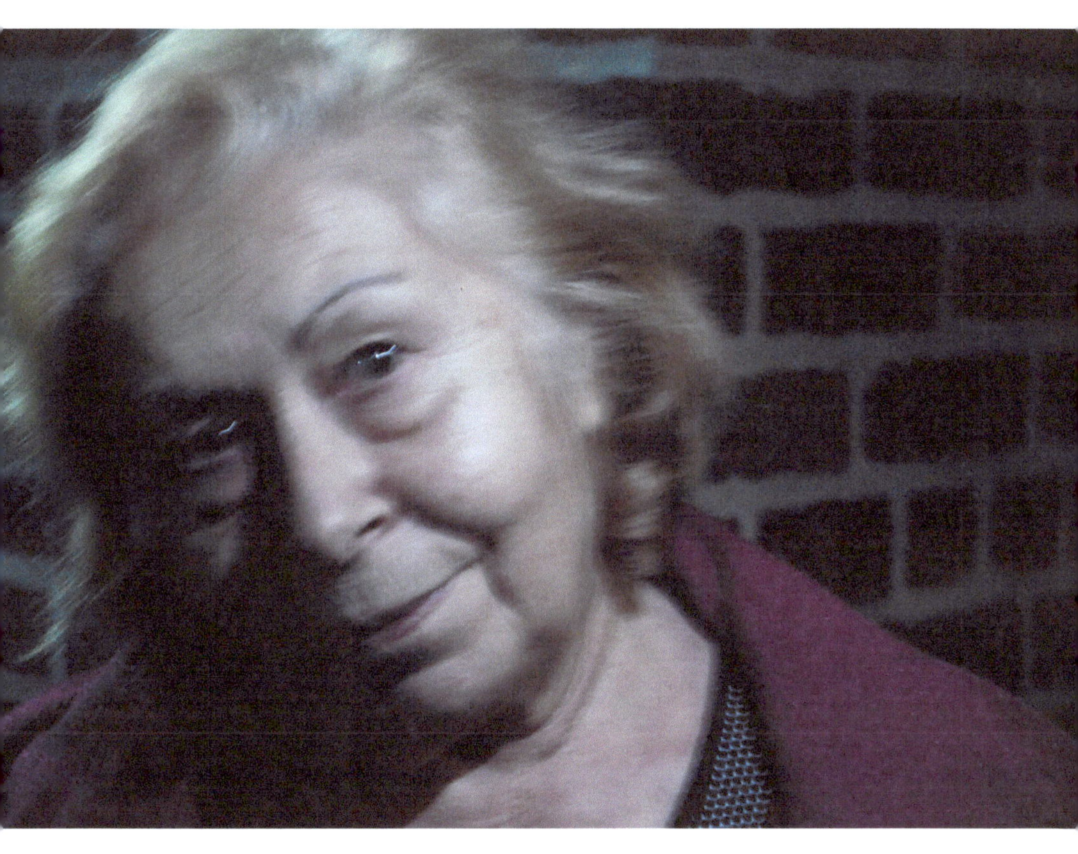

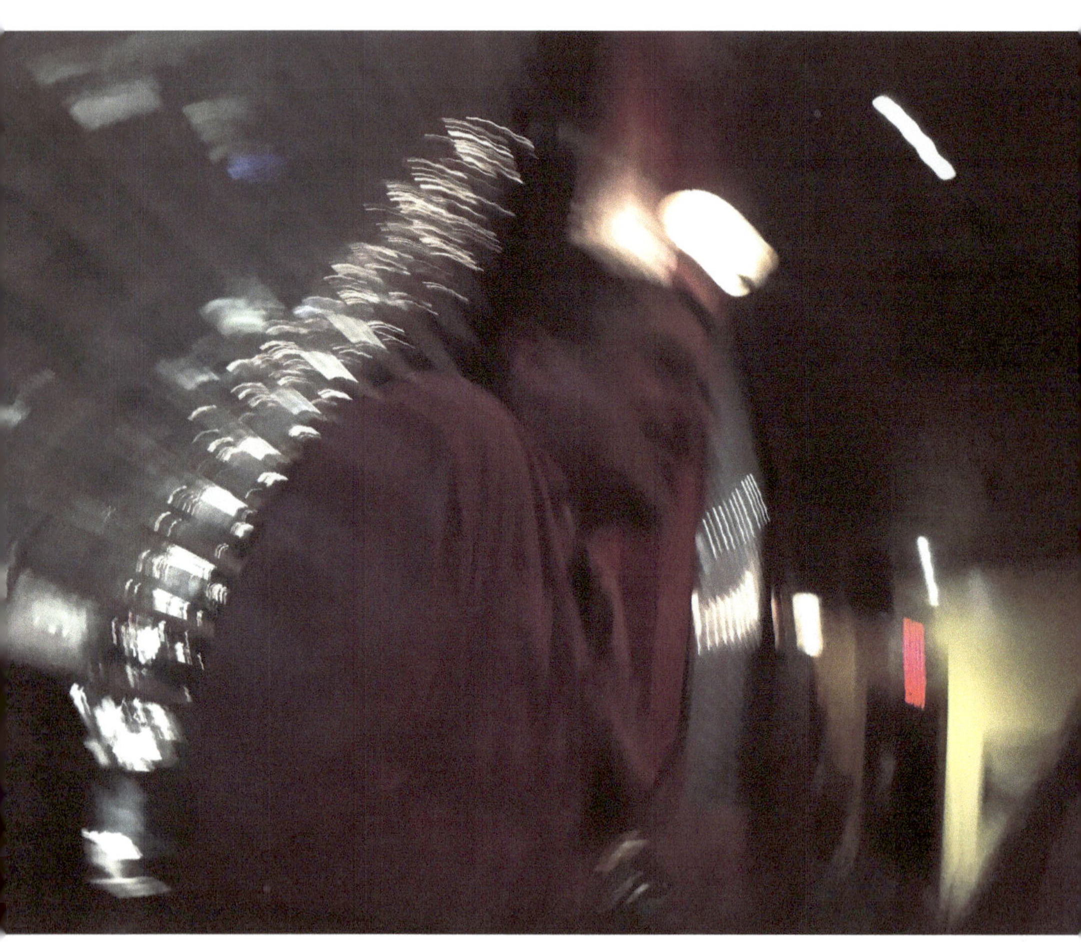

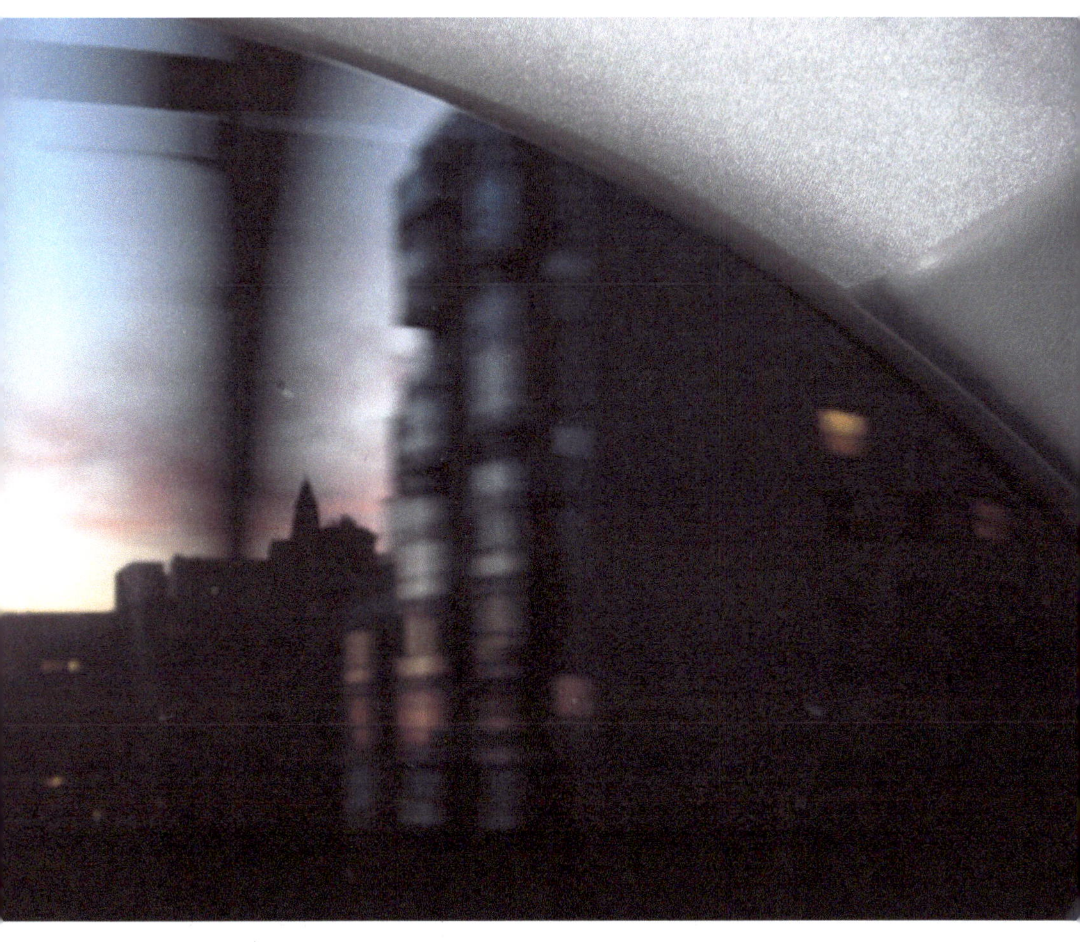

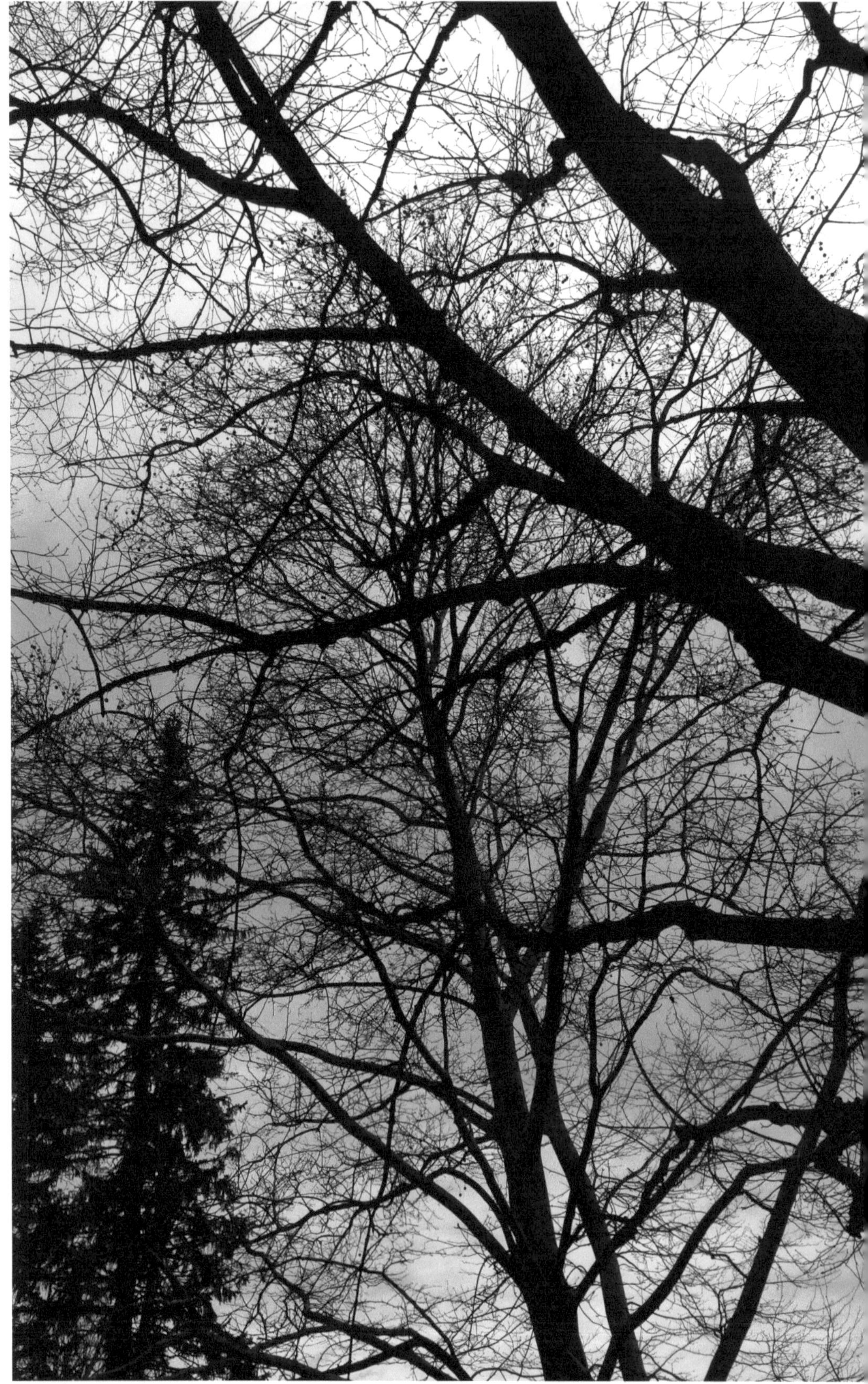

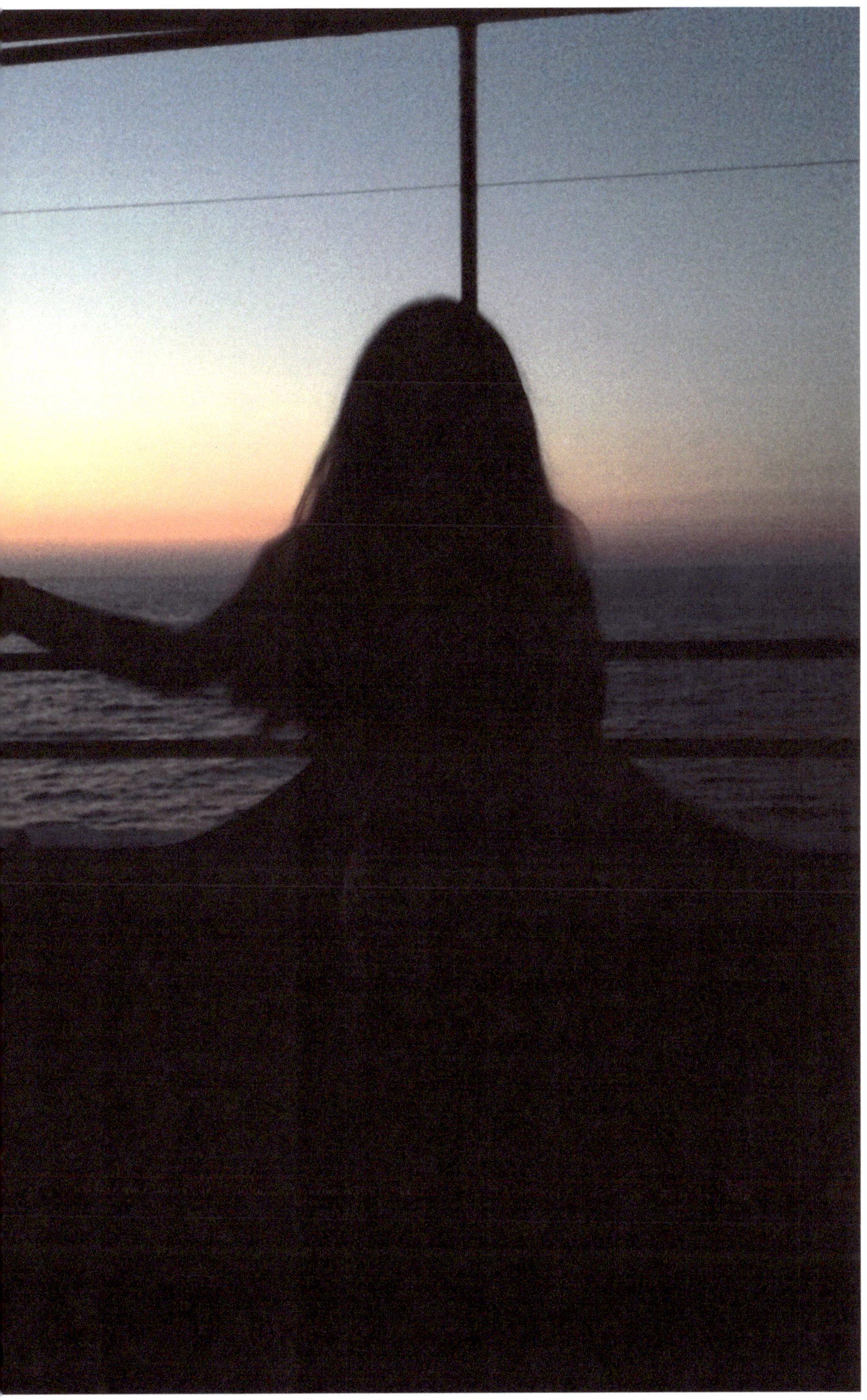

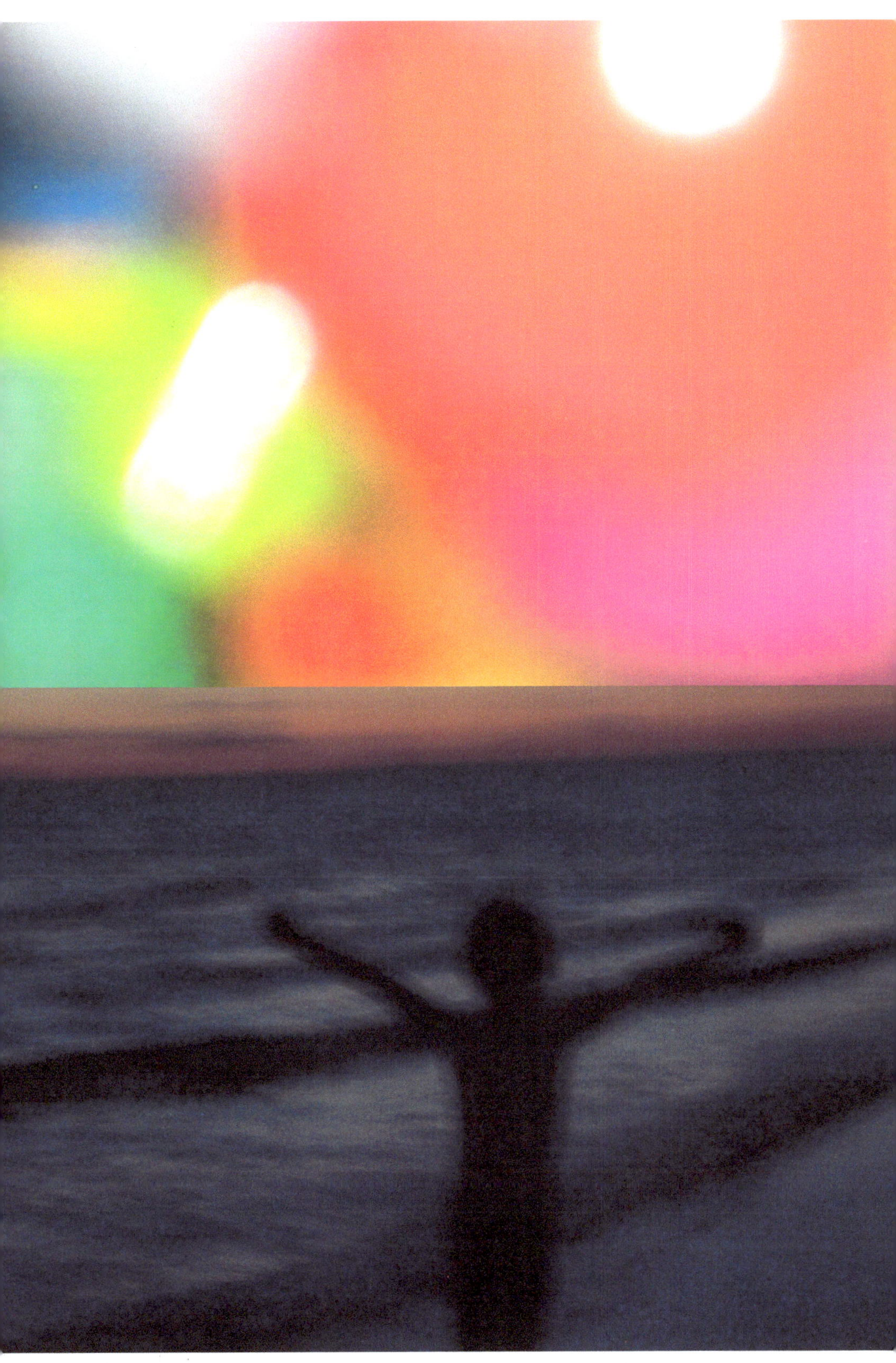

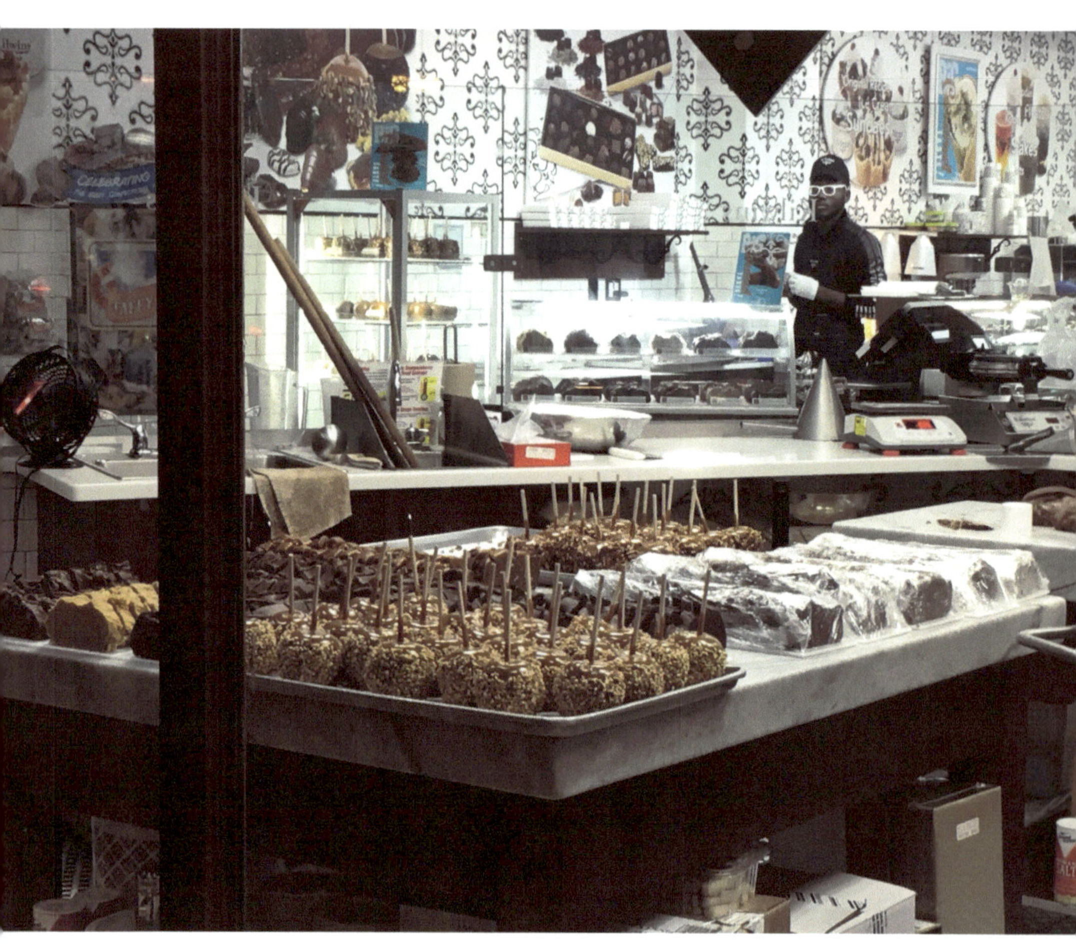
CELEBRATING

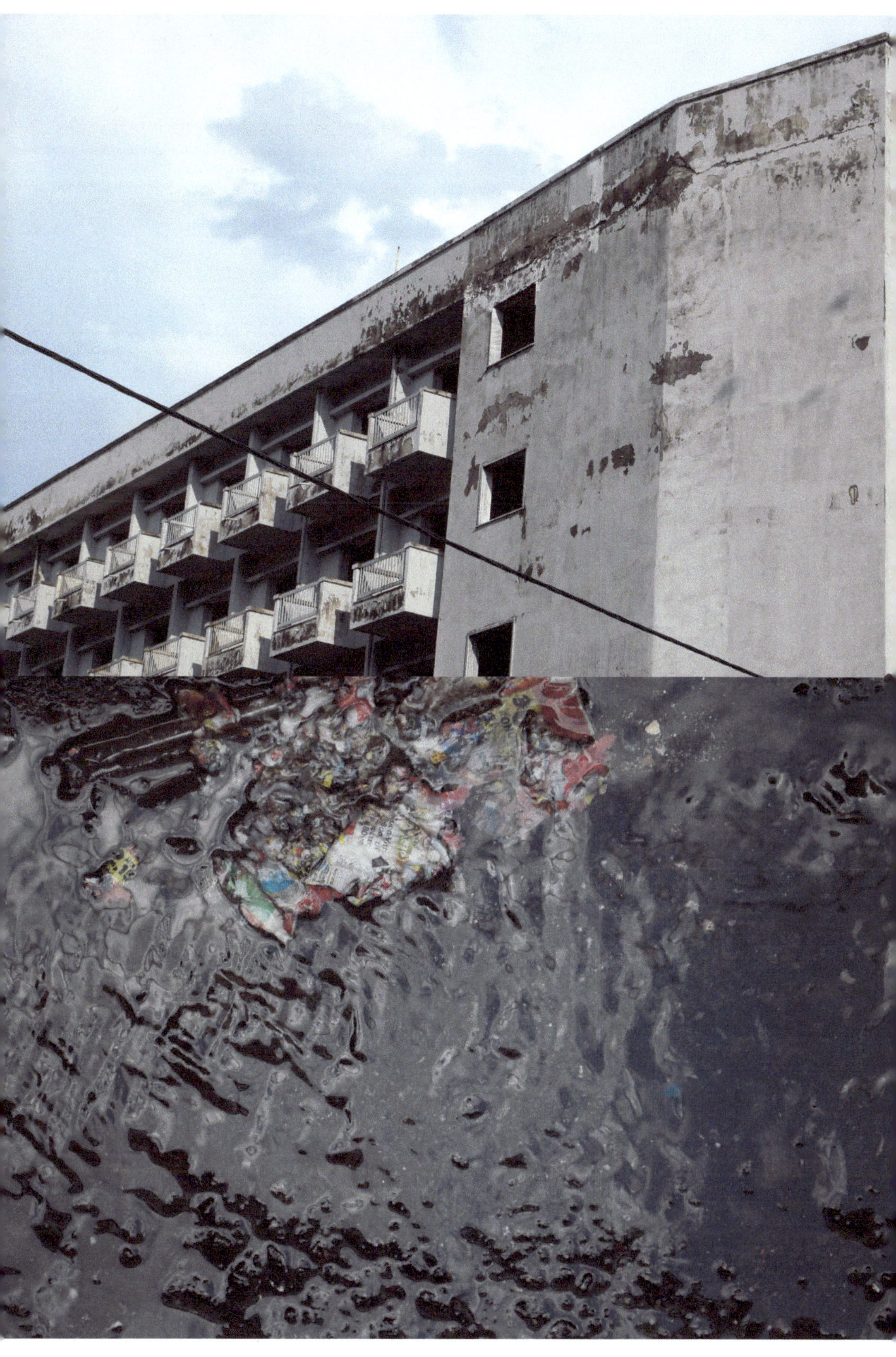

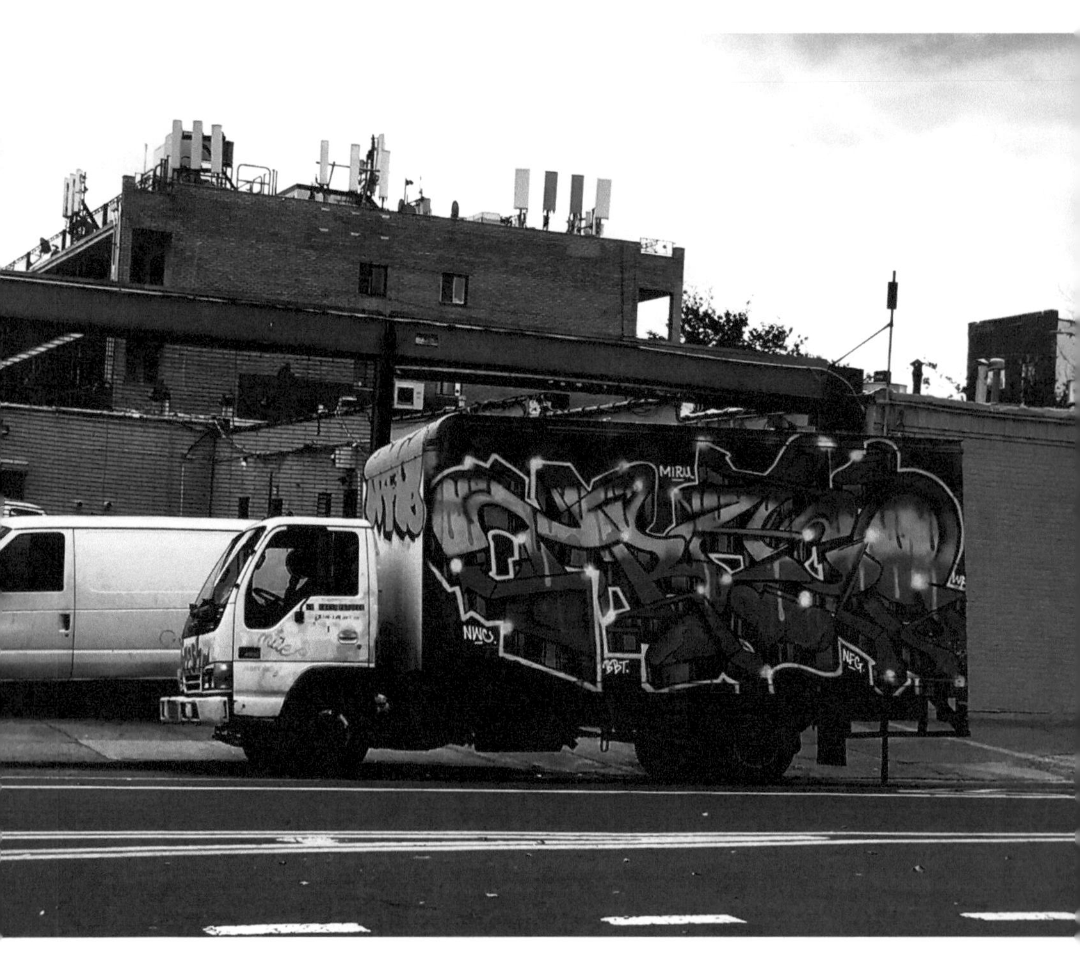
MIRU
NWC.
BBT.
NFG.

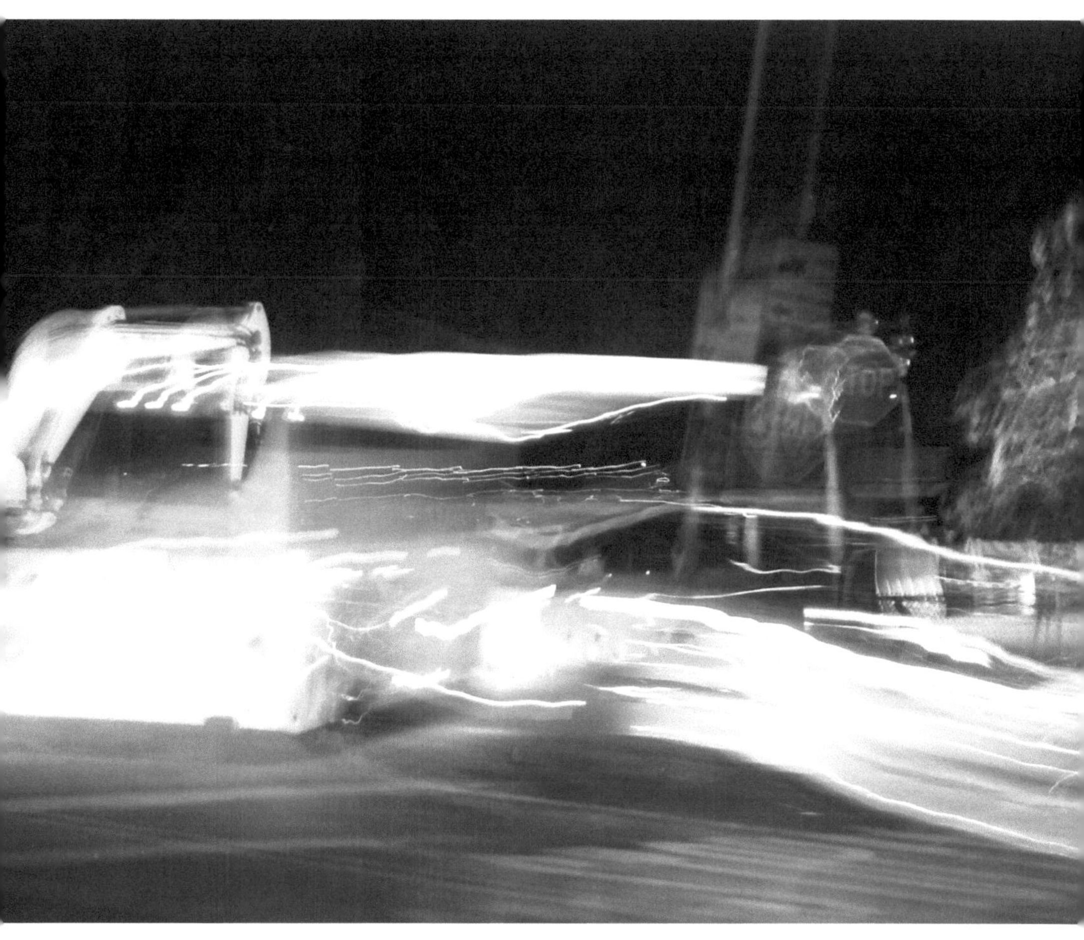

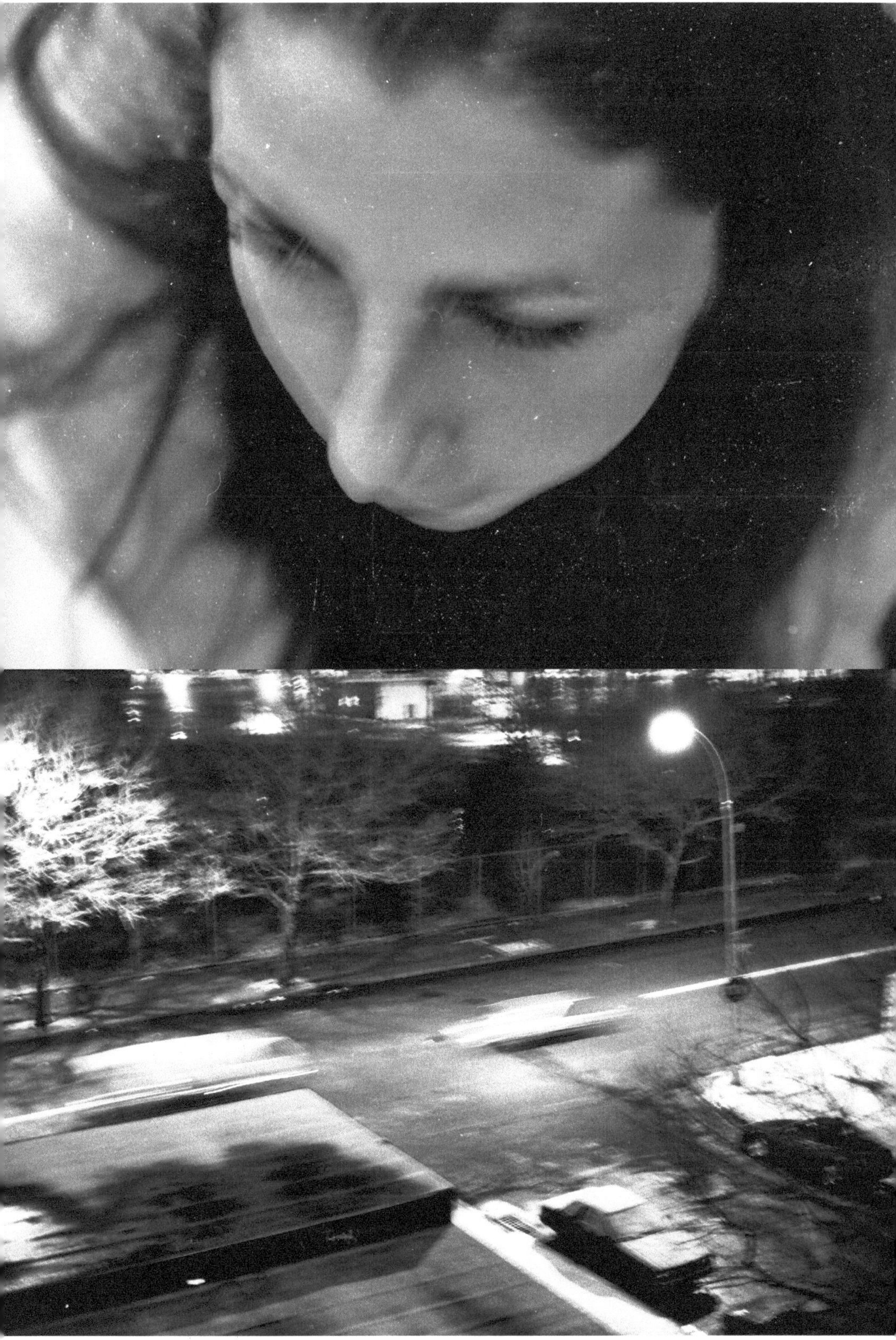

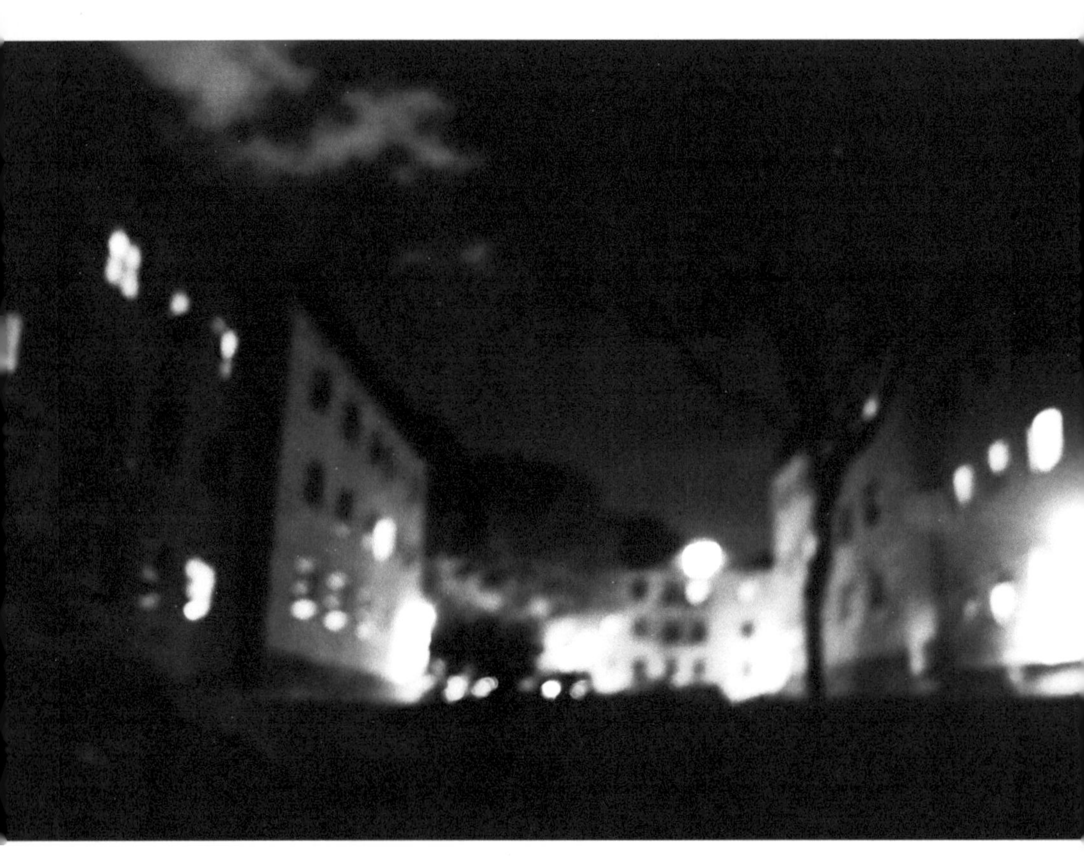

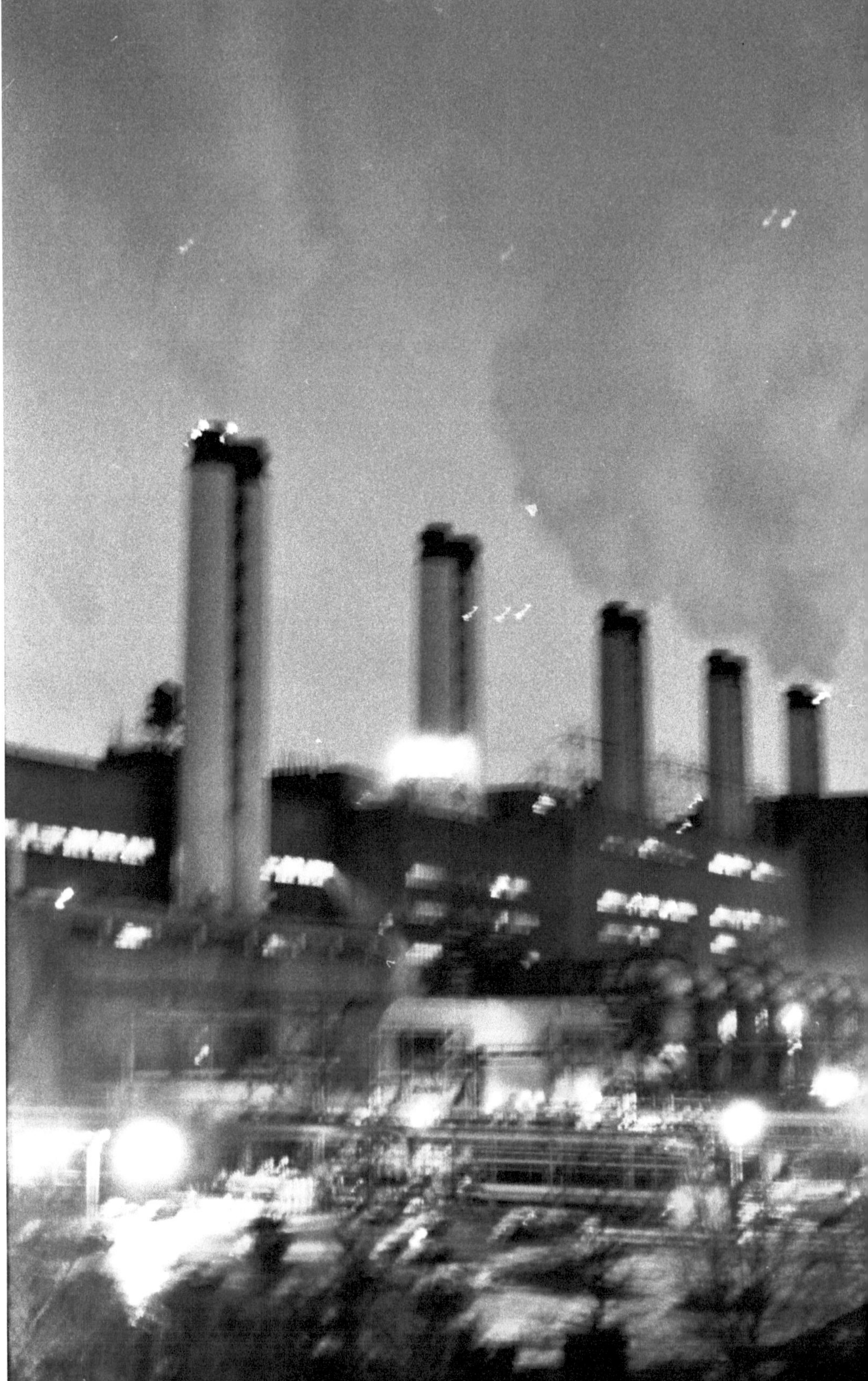

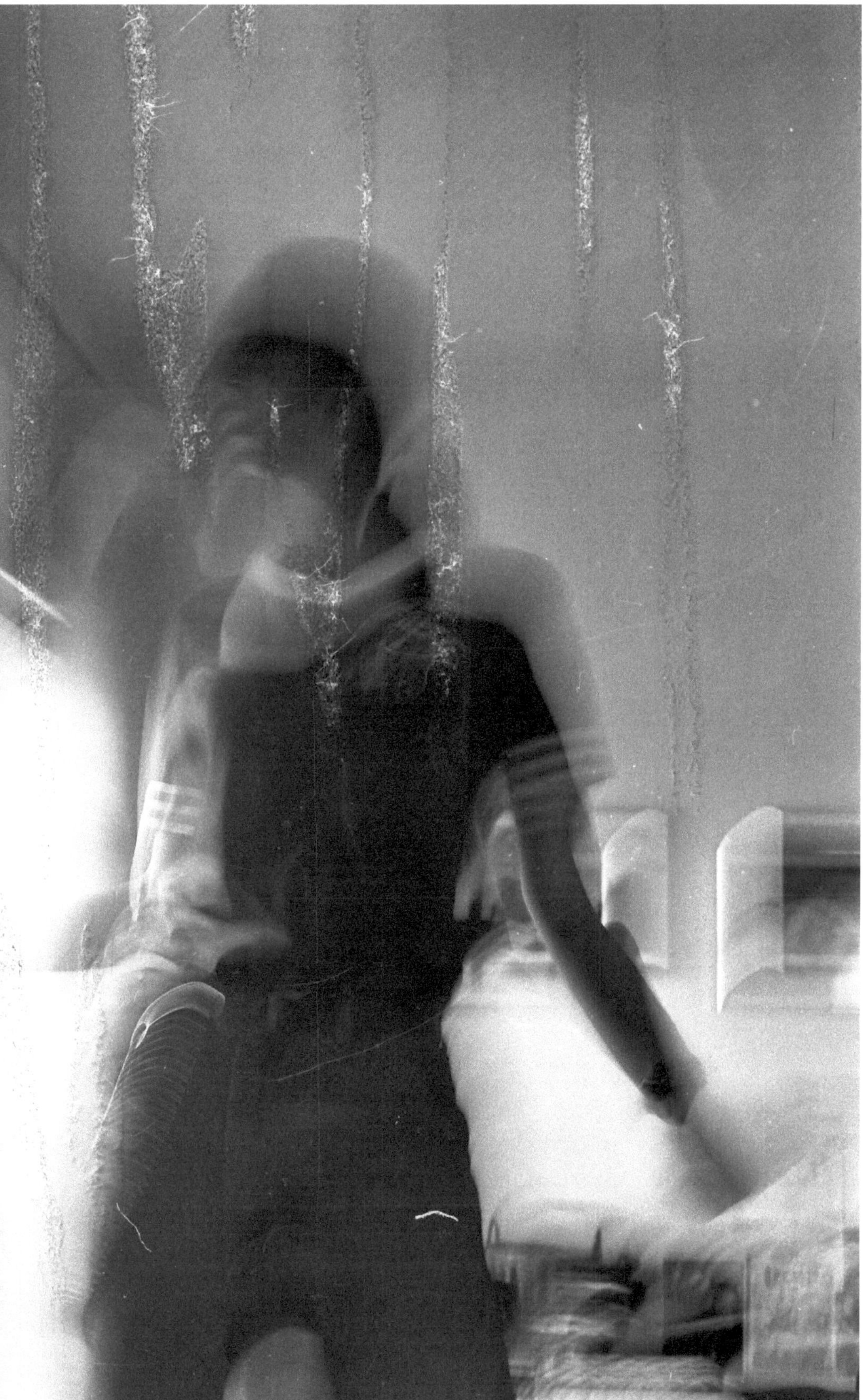

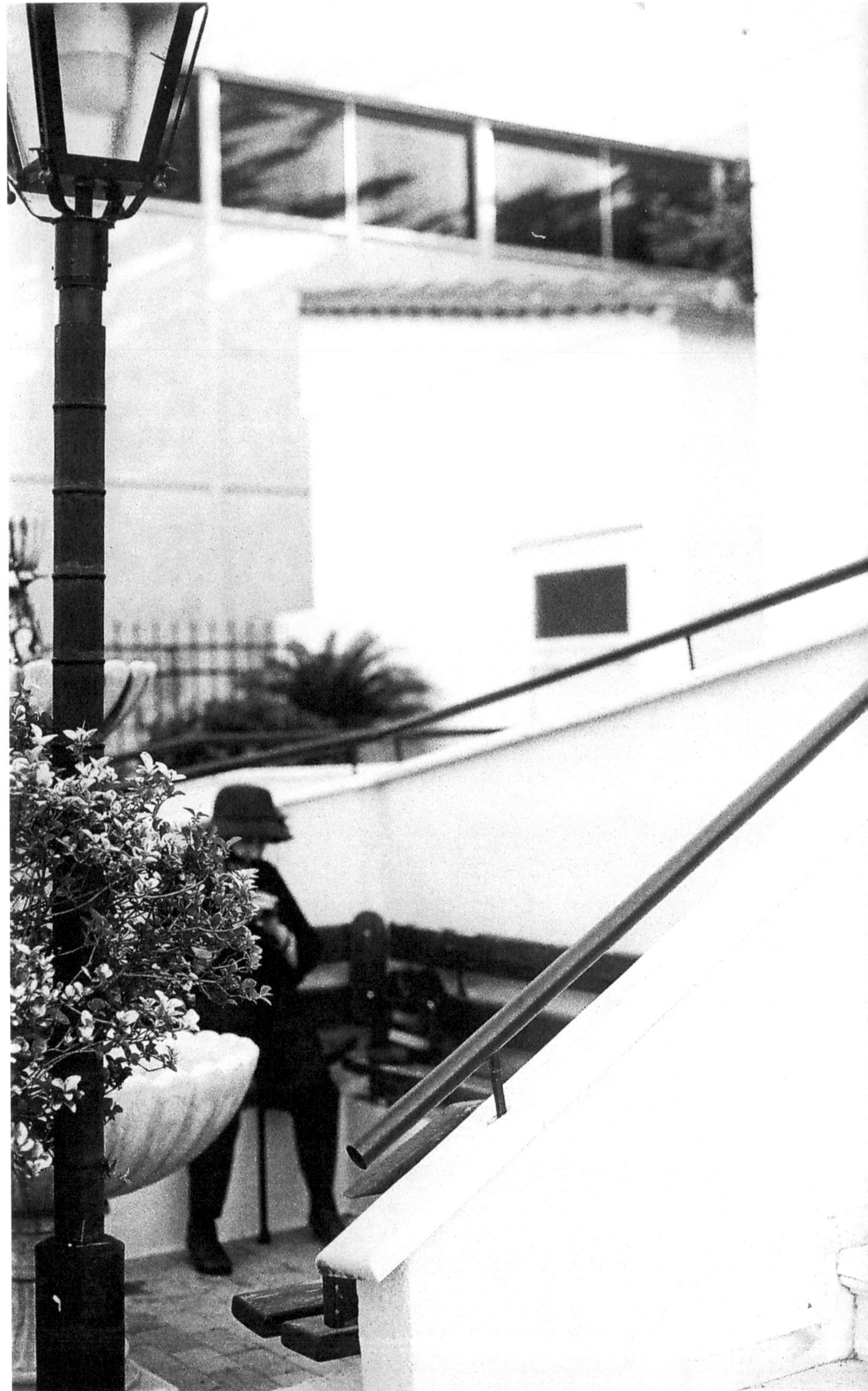

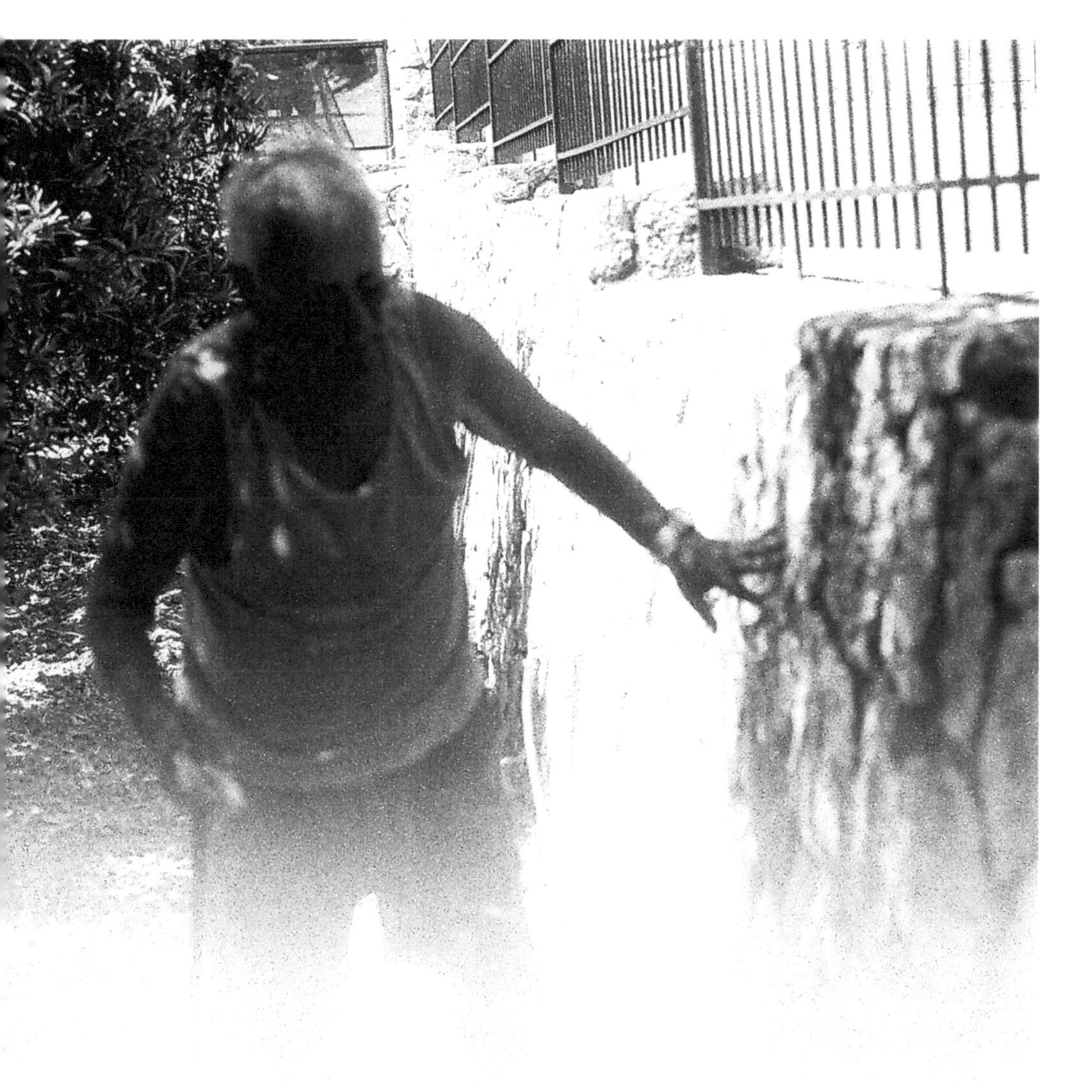

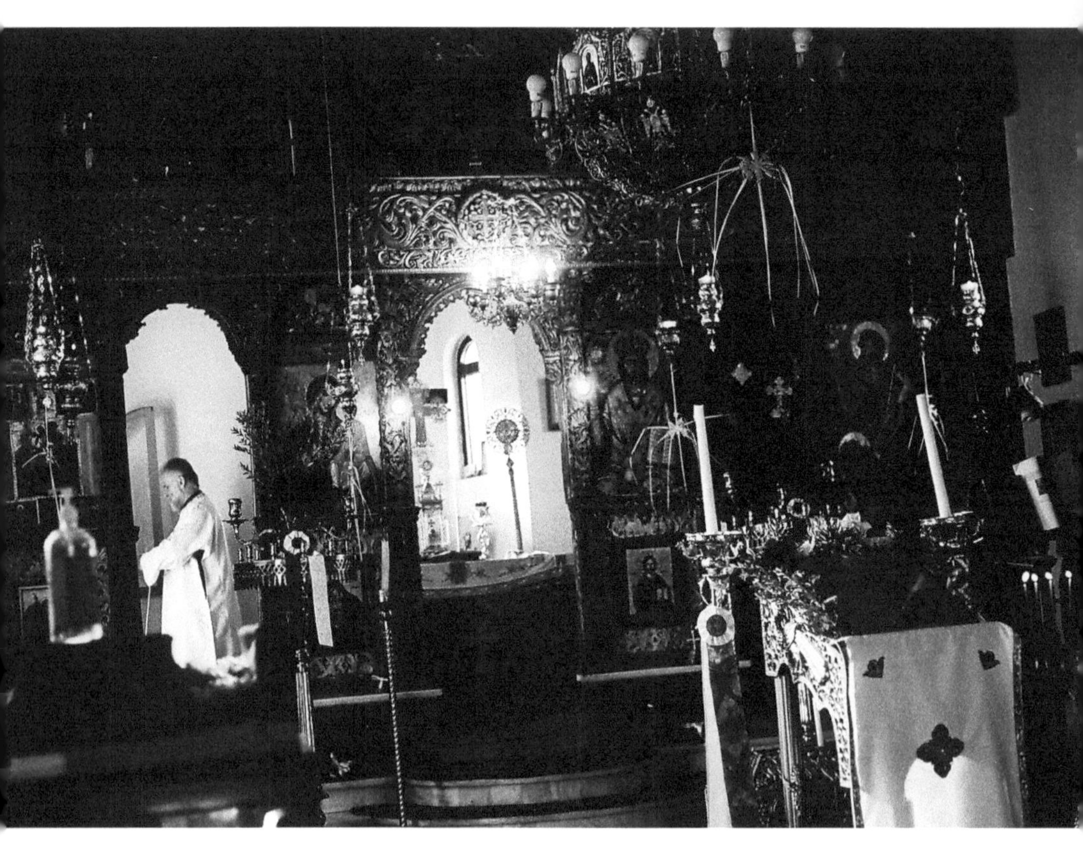

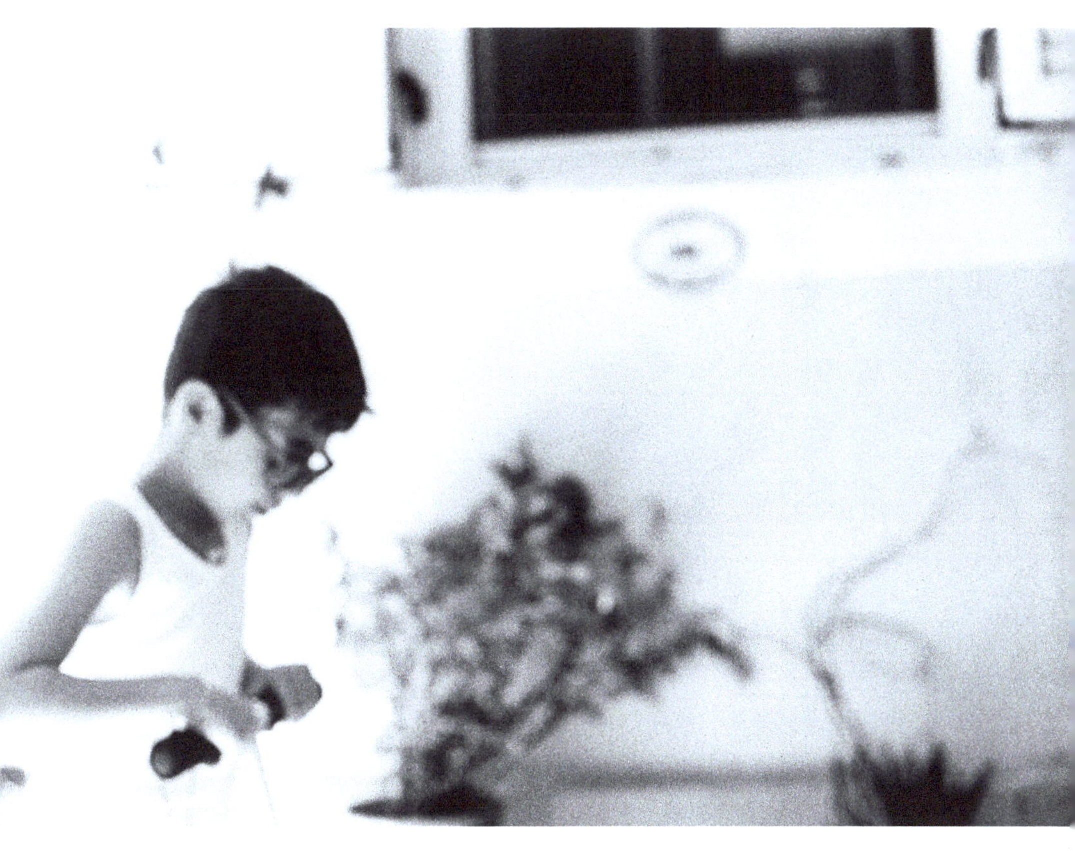

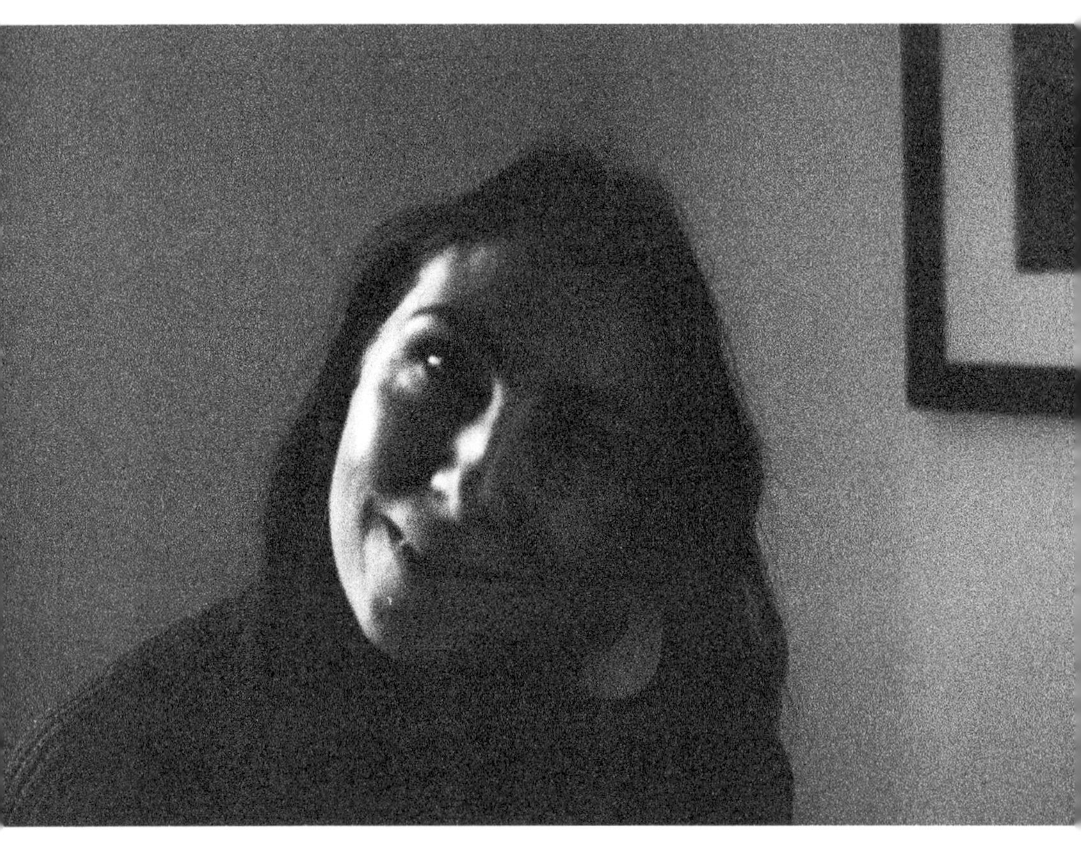

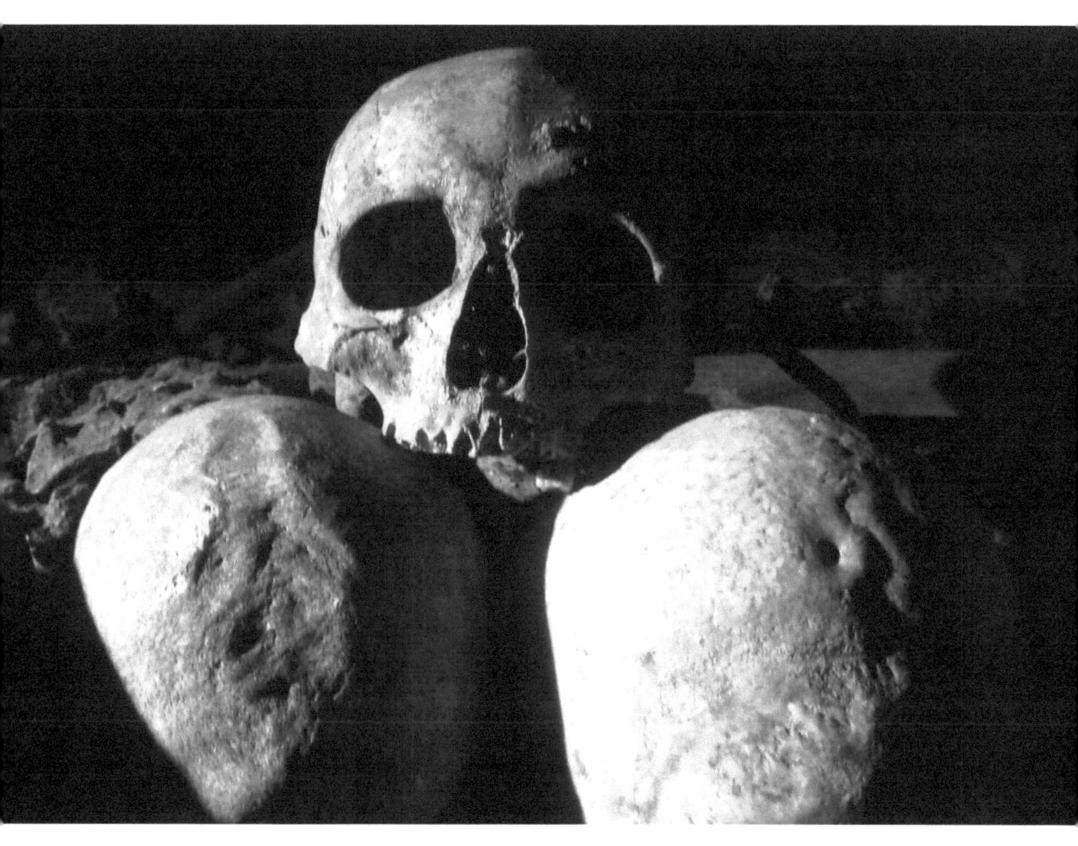

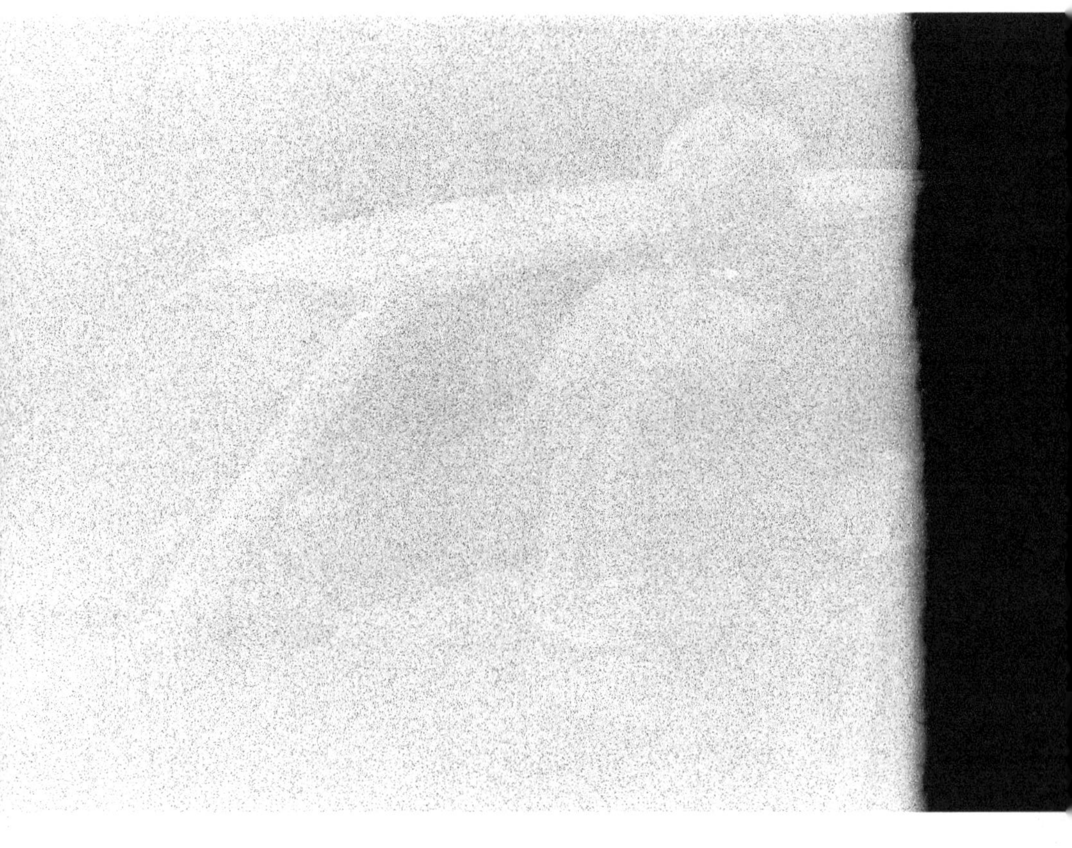

PHOTO INDEX

ONE /

15 / Self Portrait, Columbus, OH, 2019
/ Beastie Boys concert screen, McCarren Park Pool, Brooklyn, NY, 2007

17 / Graffiti, Exarcheia, Athens, Greece, 2021
/ Refugee apartment block, Dourgouti, Neos Kosmos, Athens, Greece, 2022

20 / Refugee apartment block, Dourgouti, Neos Kosmos, Athens, Greece, 2022
/ Graffiti, 5 Pointz, LIC, Queens, NY, 2010

21 / Οδός Νούμαν, Refugee apartment building, Dourgouti, Neos Kosmos, Athens, Greece, 2022 / Graffiti, 5 Pointz, LIC, NY, 2010

23 / Musicians, Xanthi, Greece, 2009
/ Marine Terrace Houses, Astoria, Queens, NY, 2022

25 / Smokestacks, Steubenville, Ohio, 2023
/ Smokestacks, Steubenville, Ohio, 2023

28 / Woman, Zola, Kefalonia, Greece, 2021
/ Birds, Refugee apartments, Dourgouti, Neos Kosmos, Athens, Greece, 2022

29 / Panagiotis, Zola, Kefalonia, Greece, 2021
/ Parthenon Marbles, Acropolis Museum, Athens Greece, 2021

31 / Seagull over the Ionian Sea, Greece, 2021
/ Graffiti, Dourgouti, Neos Kosmos, Athens, Greece, 2022

33 / Anaïs, Ventnor, New Jersey, 2020
/ Savva, Ventnor, New Jersey, 2020

35 / Windows & Shutters, Dourgouti, Athens, Greece, 2022
/ Seagulls over the Aegean Sea, Greece, 2016

38 / Refugee apartment block, Dourgouti, Athens, Greece, 2022
/ Woman, Zola, Kefalonia, Greece, 2021

39 / Gerasimos, Zola, Kefalonia, Greece, 2021
/ Refugee apartment buildings, Dourgouti, Athens, Greece, 2022

41 / Hell's Gate Bridge, Astoria, Queens, NY, 2020
/ Greek national water polo team cap, Dafni, Athens, Greece, 2017

43 / Laundromat, Paris, France, 2009
/ Grandmother's house planks, Zola, Kefalonia, Greece, 2016

46 / Girl with Bird Cage, Dourgouti, Athens, Greece, 2022
/ Refugee housing, Dourgouti, Athens, Greece, 2022

48 / Refugee housing, Dourgouti, Neos Kosmos, Athens, Greece, 2022
/ Apartment building, Dourgouti, Neos Kosmos, Athens, Greece, 2022
"Στον κόσμο των αφεντικών είμαστε όλοι ξένοι" (in the world of bosses, we are all strangers), outside refugee housing,

50 / Dourgouti, Neos Kosmos, Athens, Greece, 2022
/ Apartment building entrance, Dourgouti, Neos Kosmos, Athens, Greece, 2022

51 / Apartment building entryway, Dourgouti, Athens, Greece, 2022
/ Apartment building, Dourgouti, Athens, Greece, 2022

53 / Meters & Pipes, Dourgouti, Neos Kosmos, Athens, Greece, 2022
/ Savva on Kotso's Stoop, Zola, Kefalonia, Greece, 2021

55 / Anaïs, Columbus, OH, 2018
/ Grandmother's house planks, Zola, Kefalonia, Greece, 2016

/ TWO

73 / Magda at Notara 26 Squat, Exarcheia, Athens, Greece, 2021
/ Grandmother's house planks, Zola, Kefalonia, Greece, 2016

75 / Graffiti, Flisvos Waterfront, Palaio Faliro, Athens, Greece, 2019
/ Beastie Boys, Brooklyn, NY, 2007

77 / Jack at the Pump, Flatbush, Brooklyn, 2018
/ Young dancer, Columbus, OH, 2019

79 / Heart Shadow, Columbus, OH, 2019
/ Graffiti, Exarcheia, Athens, Greece, 2021

81 / Lights on the Avenue, Astoria, Queens, NY, 2019
/ Arcade, Columbus, OH 2021

83 / Matchbox Cars, Columbus, OH, 2019
/ Savva, Columbus, OH, 2016

86 / Road Sign, Asyrmatos social housing project, Athens, Greece, 2021
/ Graffiti, 5 Pointz, LIC, NY, 2013

87 / 5 Pointz Doorway, 5 Pointz, LIC, NY, 2010
/ Salon, Hanoi, Vietnam, 2010

89 / Merchants at the Bazaar, Xanthi, Greece, 2016
/ Water Woman, Xanthi, Greece, 2016

91 / Ice Cream, Barcelona, Spain, 2015
/ Candy stand, Mexico City, Mexico, 2019

93 / Embrace, Columbus, OH, 2013
/ First Home, Columbus, OH, 2014

95 / Savva & Fotis, Kavouri, Athens, 2017
/ Foot of the Bed, Columbus, OH, 2016

97 / Arcade, Columbus, OH, 2021
/ Graffiti, Zola, Kefalonia, Greece, 2021

99 / Fishing Nets, Astakos, Greece, 2021
/ Elli in the Terrace, Astoria, Queens, NY, 2019

101 / Friend-drunk, LIC, Queens, NY, 2018
/ View of a New Love, Queensbridge, NYC, 2010

103 / Winter Trees, Columbus, OH, 2021
/ When the Spirit Moves Her, Samos, Greece, 2017

106 / Film Magic, location unknown, 2023
/ Savva's Dance, St. Pete Beach, FL, 2020

107 / Dressed for the Part, Chicago, IL, 2017
/ Lights, Columbus, OH, 2021

110 / Apartment Building, Xanthi, Greece, 2021
/ After the Rain, Xanthi, Greece, 2021

111 / 21st Avenue Truck, Astoria, Queens, NY, 2017
/ 21st Street Truck, Astoria, Queens, NY, 2017

114 / Magda, Astoria, Queens, NY, 1993
/ The Avenue, Astoria, Queens, NY, 2018

115 / Nostos, Marine Terrace Houses, Astoria, Queens, NY, 2020
/ There is A Stillness, Astoria, Queens, NY, 2020

117 / Con Edison Smokestacks, Astoria, Queens, NY, 1993
/ Ghosts in Sunlight, Astoria, Queens, NY, 1994

119 / Resting, Xanthi, Greece, 2022
/ Kotso and the Wall, Zola, Kefalonia, Greece, 2021

121 / Pater Andrea, Zola, Kefalonia, Greece, 2021
/ Savva Scoots the Village, Zola, Kefalonia, Greece, 2021

123 / Magda, Columbus, OH, 2016
/ 3 Skulls, Catacombs, Paris, France, 2009

125 / Film Magic, location unknown, 2021
/ Film Magic, location unknown, 2023

NOTES

ONE /

Epigraphs /

The opening epigraph and intention set by George Kouvaros is from his book *The Old Greeks: Photography, Cinema, Migration* (UWA Publishing, 2018).

The modified Jack Halberstam epigraph is from the introduction "The Wild Beyond: With and for the Undercommons" in Stefano Harney and Fred Moten's *The Undercommons: Fugitive Planning & Black Study* (Minor Compositions, 2013).

the Magdalene /

The words *"city flesh"* are indebted to Wanda Coleman's phrase "labor in this city flesh, neon womb, mother cement," from a poem I have loved, but have been unable to relocate.

For a discussion of what "staying" implies see Saidiya Hartman's *Lose Your Mother: A Journey Along the Atlantic Slave Route* (Farrar, Straus, Giroux, 2007).

I found art kinship in Dionne Brand. She describes cartographers as artists and poets, as I had named the Magdalene. We share many aesthetic sensibilities via language; she writes of bodies of water meeting in a "wet blue embrace" and "the interminable waiting" and musty paper smells of colonial buildings that I recall so well as the smells and endless waiting that marked the long hours spent in Greek government offices and public assistance interviews that plagued my girlhood.

Nostos /

The words *"project projected"* engage with Fred Moten's poem "the gramsci project" in *The Little Edges* (Wesleyan University Press, 2015).

The ceiling /

For more on errant paths to what might be see Saidiya Hartman's definition of wayward in *Wayward Lives, Beautiful Experiments: Intimate Histories of Riotous Black Girls, Troublesome Women, and Queer Radicals* (W.W. Norton & Company, 2019).

The passage *"Here, now, I'm in those blessed recesses of memory"*, and its mood, pays homage to the resonances between my girlhood memories and James Baldwin's treatment of light and memory in the essay "Letter from a

Region in My Mind" (The New Yorker November 17, 1962) in which Baldwin talks about his sensations, and the quality of light filtering into his childhood apartment in Harlem: "The sunlight came into the room with the peacefulness one remembers from rooms in one's early childhood – a sunlight encountered later only in one's dreams."

The idea of "time held" is from Saidiya Hartman's "Afterword: A Room with History" in Dionne Brand's *A Map to the Door of No Return* (Picador, 2024).

"Ordinariness opening up spaces inside" is modified from Saidiya Hartman's "Afterword: A Room with History" in Dionne Brand's *A Map to the Door of No Return,* in which she discusses history and grief in Brand's work.

The concept of the *"nonplace"* and the possibilities it elicits is drawn from Fred Moten and Stefano Harney's description of the undercommons in *The Undercommons: Fugitive Planning Black Study.*

/ TWO

Epigraphs /

The epigraph opening part two is from Maggie Nelson's *The Argonauts* (Graywolf Press, 2015). I also wrote the same poem again and again, the revisitations Maggie Nelson speaks of, and the same-ish photographs. The abiding, recurring questions, worked out in text, photography, and collage as devices of art and self-making.

Brian Blanchfield's words are excerpted from a conversation between himself and Maggie Nelson titled "From Importunate to Meretricious, With Love: Conversation with Brian Blanchfield" in Maggie Nelson's *Like Love: Essays and Conversations* (Graywolf Press, 2024).

The epigraph "If they ask you, tell them we were flying" is from Stefano Harney and Fred Moten's *The Undercommons: Fugitive Planning & Black Study.*

Motherwit /

The verse of *Motherwit* first appeared in a text painting from 2018 with the same title, and was previously published in *Magda Parasidis: Ghosts in Sunlight* (Otterbein University: 2020).

Uni, or Every day the End of Something /

The second part of the title, *"Every day the End of Something"* is rooted in Jack

Halberstam's language in the introduction "The Wild Beyond: With and for the Undercommons", from Stefano Harney and Fred Moten's *The Undercommons: Fugitive Planning & Black Study.*

This poem was built thinking about the imagery of the sea urchin, as it is so common in Mediterranean waters and feels connected to my childhood. Learning more about the life cycles of sea urchins solidified the synchronicity of the reference. The following narrative gems are from a short PBS documentary, *Sea Urchins Pull Themselves Inside Out to be Reborn:*

"Having survived the long odds of youth, it's now practically immortal."
"A microscopic adult urchin is growing inside its own teenage self."
(https://www.youtube.com/watch?v=ak2xqH5h0YY):

The phrase *"our eyes fill with a wet history"* is borrowed from Kawai Strong Washburn's *Sharks in the Time of Saviors* (Picador, 2021).

"I steal back my body" is drawn from Saidiya Hartman's, *Wayward Lives, Beautiful Experiments: Intimate Histories of Riotous Black Girls, Troublesome Women, and Queer Radicals* : "It was a manner of walking that threatened to undo the city, steal back the body, break all the windows."

The couplet of "*mutual melancholy*" is from Zadie Smith's *Intimations: Six Essays* (Penguin Books, 2020).

In my treatment of historical time, the phrase *"departure anticipated and implied"* and *"ongoing"* are in conversation with Saidiya Hartman's reflections on the durative tense in Brand's writing: "The durative conveys the character of the continuing, incomplete, and the ongoing." Further discussing Brand's philosophy of time, Hartman writes "Leaving – gerund, ongoing, durative condition. To leave – infinite and anticipated, recurring, to leave again – again is implied, though not explicitly stated." See Saidiya Hartman's analysis in *Afterword: A Room with History* in Dionne Brand's, *A Map to the Door of No Return: Notes to Belonging.*

The phrase *"the structures we inhabit, inhabit us"* appears in Jack Halberstam's introduction "The Wild Beyond: With and for the Undercommons" in Stefano Harney and Fred Moten's *The Undercommons: Fugitive Planning & Black Study.*

The Block /
The Block first appeared as a text photograph by the same name in the series *Ghosts in Sunlight* from 2018, and was previously published in *Magda Parasidis: Ghosts in Sunlight.*

Makers /
"I who exceed and by exceeding escape" is borrowed from Stefano Harney and Fred Moten's *The Undercommons: Fugitive Planning & Black Study.*

Love Letter /
In *Love Letter,* the following beloved thinkers are referenced:

The phrase *"here, on the edge of everything"* is from Kelly Hayes & Mariame Kaba, *Let This Radicalize You: Organizing and the Revolution of Reciprocal Care* (Haymarket Books, 2023).

The tag *"will wuz here"* belongs to a childhood comrade from Marine Terrace Housing, in Astoria, Queens, NY.

The phrase *"true wild"* is informed by Jack Halberstam theorizing wildness in *The Queer Art of Failure* (Duke University Press, 2011) and in the introduction *The Wild Beyond: With and for the Undercommons* in Stefano Harney and Fred Moten's *The Undercommons: Fugitive Planning & Black Study.*

The concept of *"inner authority"* invokes the work of Phil Stutz in *The Tools: Transform Your Problems into Courage, Confidence, and Creativity* by Phil Stutz and Barry Michels (Spiegel & Grau, 2012).

The phrase *"the word conspire means breathe together"* originates in Robin Wall Kimmerer's B*raiding Sweetgrass: Indigenous Wisdom, Scientific Knowledge, and the Teachings of Plants* (Milkweed Editions, 2013).

The phrase *"black balm of late night"* belongs to Kawai Strong Washburn in *Sharks in the Time of Saviors.*

The line *"remembering together what has not yet been"* is modified from Maggie Nelson's response to Rosi Braidotti's "nomadic remembering" and her phraseology "we will have been free." Nelson writes, "what kind of temporal abundance allows us to remember what has not yet been?" in *On Freedom: Four Songs of Care and Constraint* (Graywolf, 2021).

With and For /
The title *"With and For"* comes from Stefano Harney and Fred Moten's *The Undercommons: Fugitive Planning & Black Study,* as does the idea of an *"outcast mass intellectuality."*

The idea of a group of wayward young people organizing in such a way that they are *"galvanizing the think that would endure and matter"* is form Saidiya Hartman's *Wayward Lives, Beautiful Experiments: Intimate Histories of Riotous Black Girls, Troublesome Women, and Queer Radicals.*

"I remake my place in the world, in your company" is modified from a George Kouvaros text in *The Old Greeks: Photography, Cinema, Migration.*

The line *"before the long discipline of making sense of what one has seen"* is indebted to John Burnside's discussion of that which is required after the artist/anarchist returns from his liberatory flights in *On Henry Miller: Or, How to Be an Anarchist* (Princeton University Press, 2018).

"On the way to another place altogether" is from Jack Halberstam's introduction to Stefano Harney and Fred Moten's *The Undercommons: Fugitive Planning & Black Study.*

The poem references the *"noise of objection"* from Dionne Brand's preface to *A Map to the Door of No Return,* but also Jack Halberstam's idea that "cacophony and noise tell us that there is a wild beyond to the structures we inhabit and that inhabit us" from the introduction to *The Undercommons: Fugitive Planning & Black Study.*

"Friend-drunk" is from the Danez Smith's "how many of us have them?" in *Homie: Poems* (Graywolf Press, 2020).

The phrase *"an everyday choreography of the possible"* is from Saidiya Hartman's *Wayward Lives, Beautiful Experiments: Intimate Histories of Riotous Black Girls, Troublesome Women, and Queer Radicals.*

AFTERWORD

The collection of photographic diptychs in *One/Two* has emerged as a personal history of seeing, making, and collecting images. "I'd like to meet someone whose passage through life has happened to an essential self, and not been just a series of lives happening to a series of selves," writes Sarah Manguso in *300 Arguments.*[1] Curating the image associations in *One/Two* has been an archival project of sorts, in that it documents a continuity of making pictures and aesthetic connections. It is a thread to that essential self Manguso wonders after, at least to an aesthetic one. My inheritances, history, and aesthetic sensibility are implicated in every picture and pairing. This variety of what Maggie Nelson calls "enmeshments," chart a way of seeing the spheres of a life - private, social, political, and spiritual - via the methodology of this project.[2] Working with my visual attractions and attachments affords me access to rarely visited parts of memory, that mash up of collected images that curate an internal narrative, and that have prompted the writing of the poems.

Taped pairs of photographs have a long-standing presence on my studio wall. The visual juxtapositions have been a way to commune with myself, as disparate photographs attach to one another with the inevitability of belonging together, creating a new work of its own insistent invention. One of the delights of this way of making has been to recognize that the image's infusion with a kind of life force is the criteria that it desired to be collected, as if it would not, could not, remain in piles on the work table. The diptychs are not representations of the unheralded miracle of the good picture, but moments when failed photographs find their purpose, or when a photograph continues in its becoming in relation to another. Some images fuse together, others complete one another, while others still, resonate for their mood or humor. On how she knows a piece is done, the artist Sarah Lucas says, "It jumps to life. Becomes more than the sum of its parts. Has a character. Is something seen for the first time."[3] In other words, the maker, directed by her own discretion, recognizes the completion of the process of becoming when the object is emanating its own presence. The encounter with this presence when pulsing pairs unite is a balm, and the swell of collected images in the studio has something of the abundant; a promise of the possibility of making something of one's intuitions.

In responding to my own desire to salvage certain resonant photographs, despite not being able to place them in the organizing container of a "project" until now, an active rejection of disposability emerged in my studio practice. I recognize the thrift in photographer Moyra Davey, when she recounts rummaging through her archive with "the ambivalent gratification of rediscovering forgotten selves." She asks herself why she doesn't just use some of the "found" photographs, and have this gesture signify "resistance to further production/consumption?"[4] The photographic collage work I continue to pursue is produced from this same gesture. If a photograph was once framed through the viewfinder as an imprint of my gaze, then it could find its way to becoming. It's essentially the poor person's frugality folded into a modality of making, and when applied to making and seeing, has unexpected results. Photographic mishaps may have aesthetic value, and distortions might make meaning more clear. The dematerialized blurred photo urges to be looked at more closely, its expression of mood more precise for its imperfection. It might offer an unsentimental way of looking and seeing from the most personal of haunts and intimacies – at the foot of a mother's bed, in a private embrace, sitting for a family portrait, or a beloved best friend in a swirl. The convergence of moods and impressions is both the stuff of the visual work and the source of the tug to bridge the aesthetic with language. Something more wanted to be made of root knots overtaking a building, while wild curls reach skyward in an Ionian gust above a fiercely centered face. Or with photographs of children and their "native joy and robustness:" my son blissed out on the beach and my daughter in her own ecstasy, as she dances the sunset away, the sky blistering pink and orange.[5]

As the diptychs accrued, and the themes of *One/Two* made themselves known, language began insistently appearing in tandem with the photographic work. In *A Map to the Door of No Return*, Dionne Brand writes, "One enters a room and history follows; one enters a room and history precedes. History is already seated in the chair in the empty room when one arrives."[6] This is the resonant effect this project has had on me, as if the photographs hold arcs of a narrative of what came before, while the visual syntax is of an ever-existing present. If the diptychs stand still in time, not of the past, or of what has been, but of an ongoing present infused with the past, with what George Kouvaros in *The Old Greeks* calls the "restless persistence of the past," then we might think of them as photographic tableaux.[7] "Tableaux have to do with story, but insofar as they are perched in time, they offer a kind of pause or suspension from it," writes Maggie Nelson in *On Freedom*.[8] It is this suspension of time/space that I could inhabit when writing the prose poems, in which the girl/woman employing nonlinear time in her narrative, addresses her adolescent friends, her children, and herself, all at once. On how we exist in time, what and how much we carry with us, who and what is the receptacle of what we carry (the images, people, places, and our own accumulation of impressions, moods, and associations),

Saidiya Hartman writes, "the synchronic inhabitation of multiple presents defines embodied experience."[9]

Inhabiting multiple presents infused with the ghosts of the past is a useful lens with which to consider the her/story of immigration and girlhood in the verses. My family and I arrived in Queens in September of 1980 from Athens. The beginning of an immigrant's life in a new country is marked by "a loss that has already occurred," having lost a mother country, for the new and unknown."[10] In *One/Two*, I revisit the places and aesthetics that recall a sense of this abiding loss. "A loss that inaugurates one's existence" is described by Saidiya Hartman in *Lose Your Mother* as "revisiting the routes that might have led to alternative presents, salvaging the dreams unrealized and defeated, crossing over to parallel lives. Loss remakes you ."[11] The aesthetic devotion to urban landscapes and their centrality in my work has been a way of making from this sense of loss, and a way of working with my inheritances as a new American. In his endless insights on photography and migration, George Kouvaros writes that we "align our own incomplete history with the history of images. The restless, never-finished engagement with images is his response to the quintessential migrant endeavor to remake one's place in the world."[12] If the sense of one's place in the world begins with the specificity of home, then the particularity of the landscape of home - for me, public housing in Astoria, Queens, situated across the street from a power plant - has been a riddle to unravel alongside the complications of migration. Beyond a way of situating myself in the world, my home and its carceral aesthetics have demanded that I develop a narrative and a politics. And I've done this exhaustively, as an educator, in the series *Ghosts in Sunlight*, and in my personal and political commitments. The art practice I've pursued since becoming a mother has largely been committed to the potential of politicizing one's privations and experiences in the service of others. But in *One/Two* there is a parallel narrative recovered, even celebrated, from the twin experiences of migration and poverty, and the dual presence of Astoria and Athens. There was more to say, this time about the poetic possibilities of the projects, and their complicity with other places on the edge via my aesthetic devotions. Along with critique, I recover passages from my notebooks that testify to the creative potential of marginal spaces:

> *The girl/child was awed by the vertiginously tall smokestacks erupting unpredictably against the sky. She was transfixed by the graffitied tags, layered and proximate, and drawn to add her own mark to the cacophony of these mashed up proxies claiming a tiny corner-canvas of the block. To say nothing of*

the buildings, the repetition of brick buildings, framed with fences, landscaped with concrete, doors numbered just so, stairwells of possibility and decadence, the dead bolt between the inside and the landing. The windows facing the street and those looking out on the avenue, framing that desolate, dangerous view imbued with the intrigue and the escapades of the outlaw. The childhood fear of the dark matured to a devotion to the most captivating hour in the hood, in all its meditative stillness. Silently watching from her bedroom, entranced, waiting for something to come into view, wholly captivated by the terrain of the nocturnal streetscape. Pondering in place, "the inside that is outside,"[13] *the private that is always public. The quiet that must be love.*

I also recovered what I'll broadly call camaraderie, understood as the experiences with people that allow us a sense of connection and shared purpose. Place shapes and forms us, and contributes to our identity, but the first generation immigrant is always aware of being from two places and belonging to neither, what Kouvaros calls the "in-betweenness" of the migrant, and her condition of "residing in the cleft."[14] But to be in a place and not entirely of it, is also one of the qualities in the life of the "other." In my corner of Astoria, Queens there were many "others": all us immigrants and all of us who were experiencing poverty with the intersection of cultural outsideness due to race or ethnicity, sexuality or ability. We all knew poverty and we all knew to be intimidated by power. But the complicities between us weren't only born of the specificity of our strain of struggle. We recognized and relished in each other's displays of dignity. The Black women on Sunday mornings with their pastel suits and hats headed to church, the beautiful teenage girl that would be picked up by a boy/man in a red convertible, the sound system in someone's trunk, the neighbor turned firefighter that would bring the firetruck to the block to show off to us kids, the young man walking home from work in a shirt and slacks – these were all openings, seeing us leave the confines of our block and venturing out there, an "us" out in the world.

Poverty is a defining experience, often accompanied by repeated and recurring trauma, as is migration, and in *One/Two*, the verses rely on the interiority of girlhood and its narrative possibilities to tell us both about the loss of a mother country, and of subsequent losses, the ones accompanied with crossing socioeconomic boundaries. In *The Blue Clerk*, Dionne Brand, as a nine year old, standing on her street, thinks to herself:

> I knew I would never live there again all my life. The thought altered the afternoon and my life, and after that I was in a hurry to leave. There was another consciousness waiting for a little girl to grow up and think future thoughts, waiting for some years to pass and some obligatory life to be lived until I would arrive here. When I was nine I left myself and entered myself.[15]

Brand knows as a girl that she will leave her village in Trinidad, more precisely, that she must leave. The grieving is before the loss, and it will go on. Its duration will mark her in the past, is marking her, has marked her, marks her still. In *A Map to the Door of No Return* she writes:

> I remember standing at the top of the street to my house when I was thirteen thinking, I will leave here and never return, I am not going to live here. Already the books in my mind were read, already I was forgetting faces and names, already all that was happening had happened. The street was a ghost.[16]

I also write about a certain girlhood at 7 or 8, at 10, at 13, at 16 or 17, the girl/woman enduring at 25, not lost at 29. The markers in the verses are the friendships lived parallel to the ongoingness of the already lost home and the maternal rift. They are love letters to the friends of childhood and adolescence, those friends that are in the present and have been in the past. She is the untamed girl-child with the boys, charting a course with the intimacy and creative possibilities of friendship at its center. She might narrate the easy camaraderie of being with the neighborhood boys, smoking and giggling over one another on the edge of the bed in her girlhood room, looking out the window onto the avenue at the unbelievably high smokestacks smoking perpetually, like tall white blunts in the sky. And themselves high - their mothers will be home from their respective sweat shops soon, but for now, the smokestacks smoke, and they along with them. They are a different kind of family, kin from the neighborhood and the block.

The kinship and opportunities to craft a self *vis-à-vis* adolescent friendships has much to do with initiations. First experiences of ecstasy and bliss were the way that I first glimpsed what "getting out" could feel like. With my mother making no progress in learning English, and the year-in and year-out appointments in public assistance offices, the only promise of a different reality was in some still abstract adult future after college and a "good job." But I could visit those places within myself that promised liberation, without permission or resources – to be my own font and my own source. It was the experience of the otherworldly – the bliss state – through communion with friends, through sex, drugs, and later through spiritual practice, that could allow me to intuit the bricks, fences, and smokestacks as sites of reverential beauty. The site of so much grief, could also be experienced as the place that came alive in dreamscapes and night flights, illuminated by street lamps, building spotlights, or helicopter beams hovering up above.

> Other and other. How did they all get together, I wonder. Not just their first and last names but the three of them. Friends, co-conspirators, co-defendants. They met as outsiders, no doubt. Outsiders to the city and outsiders in their own homes; the homes, the families that gave them the last names, the same families that gave them the first names to protect them from last names. What they did isn't clear: shoplifting, perhaps; fighting three other girls, perhaps. Anyway, three of them did whatever it was together.[17]

This description of a group of "diasporic children," friends in trouble with the law, recalls my tendency to politicize the childhood friendships I've known for the ways in which they clarify power dynamics and reveal the economic, sexual, and parental violence inside our families and mother-led households. It seemed that the places of goodness, enjoyment, revelry, or what I understood to be manifestations of freedom, were precisely in the places and with the people my people wanted to keep me safe from. The making of a political self through the camaraderie of young friendships made its way into the poetry, as did the impetus to make art out of what one has seen and experienced. The intimate space created through artistic practice – or in one's room – is a potent strategy to counter the intrusions of privacy via surveillance that so many poor and otherwise suspect populations are subjected to. Making photographs as a teenager was a first experimentation in artmaking as emancipatory practice. The picture plane was the inviolable space, a site of rupture to surveillance, propriety and control. And what's commonly known as adolescent rebellion is also an emancipatory practice when read as a practice for alternative modes of living. The politicizing potential of the sanctuary of young friendships is not unlike the theorizing of commune building and occupation culture of autonomous movements. My familiars and I certainly operated as a network of comrades, with a capacity to supply ourselves with experiences of leisure and joy with little to no money in the New York City of the 1990s, utilizing the street, the parks, public transportation and our mothers' subsidized apartments as sites for our exchanges. Money wasn't the currency that circulated among us. Our way of being together was a rehearsal for a mode of living outside of the economy and its logic, a way of occupying the city and its commons, and creating or finding ourselves in circumstances which allowed people of like-minded sensibilities to encounter one another, and sometimes coalesce.[18]

Embedded in *One/Two* is a deep investment in the semiotics of the ghetto, and what poet Billy-Ray Belcourt calls a "nod to the geographies of joy that manifest where we are trained not to see them."[19] In an effort to alchemize an interest in marginal spaces into documents of creative imagination, I've found myself dedicated to looking, and looking again, at apartment buildings, and at the phenomenon of buildings. To participate in their collectivity for me is to be left in perpetual wonderment at these colossuses, and awash in solidarity, believing in "a first-person plural"; the we bonds of the home/place I come from and every place like it. The architectural photographs in the book, even with no people in sight, are indexical markers of "a metropolis teeming with other lives.[20] I carry my own wild home with me when venturing to other people's cities, and I experience it as a homecoming of sorts to see the activities of collectivity and creative resistance played out in urban commons - on city walls, in parks, in squares, in community gardens, or in occupied areas. A quiet street on a smoldering Athenian morning feels fraught with references and semantic nudges for all the ways the street records histories of artistic practice, of political resistance, and of the migration of peoples.

It is a reliably moving experience to see expanses of graffiti in the anarchist/occupied neighborhood of Exarcheia in Athens, not only because it is a model of contestation and rupture, but because it is a collision of the aesthetics I inherited as a child riding subway trains in Queens, and those of the lost city in which I will never be native. That these two places are in conversation, or collusion, or betweenness, like myself, is a way to experience immigration that gestures toward a shared life in the undercommons. Stefano Harney and Fred Moten's influential book *The Undercommons: Fugitive Planning & Black Study* gifts us a framework of encounter in the communal activities of the undercommons, characterized by study, refusals or resistance, collective care, and creative practices.[21] The inscriptions on the walls of Exarcheia, and on those of any other place, is the testimony that networks of people are active here, and that a stranger might find belonging in the undercommons.

The Athens streetscape insists – and this has long been true – that we consider the radical, the anarchic, and the presence of those considering insurrection. An active resistance is ever-brewing: I imagine it dreamed up in the afternoon siestas following the midday meals, whose preparations started in early morning. What Robin D.G. Kelley calls "freedom dreams," outlaw culture, and an aesthetic of resistance are embroidered onto, what seems like every other wall of the city, fugitive canvases appearing less for beauty than for message.[22] The improvised and political, with no measure for propriety, just presence, are everywhere visible, lest we forget. Athens demands to be considered and debated. She is always, always reminding us of the anti-establishment and the opposition - and graffiti is her most consistent provocation.

Less readily visible in the geography of the city are the neighborhoods and the structures built to house the poor. Pilgrimages through Athens with my husband to other people's ghettos with my camera have been to unearth the geopolitical stories of displaced people in the architecture of the historic city. *One/Two* includes photographic studies of the settlement of Dourgouti, and the social housing estate of Asyrmatos, both created to accommodate Greek refugees arriving in Athens from Asia Minor in the 1920s. The country has a long relationship with displaced people in the contemporary era: Greek refugees from Asia Minor and the Black Sea region post-1922, and internal political refugees fleeing persecution during the civil war of the 1940s and throughout the junta of 1967-1974. More recently, Greece has had to address arrivals from the Balkans and the former Soviet Union, economic refugees following the global financial crisis in 2008, and the staggering numbers of Middle Eastern and African peoples searching for safe harbor on its shores. Integral to modern Greek identity is a cyclical experience of immigration, having been emigrants themselves and now finding that they are protagonists in the humanitarian imperative to receive asylum seekers and displaced peoples. This is fertile ground for anyone like myself interested in understanding the phenomenon of migration after experiencing it myself, and with an interest in how political commitments are formed as a result of our formative experiences. Roaming into neighborhoods I was primed to love because of the history of precarity they hold, or because they are on the edge, like Dourgouti and Asyrmatos, is also to experience the city as social atlas. I seek out the personal and geopolitical histories of the displaced in the apartment blocks built by the state because they collapse my story as a new American and the stories of new Greeks – a shared humanity decades apart, yet simultaneous. Their stories are also my story as long as my political loyalties and commitments aren't misplaced, or the edge isn't forgotten.

Along with Greek, the mother tongue I give my children is the self-authoring in the work I make. And the perspective the children have given me, from witnessing them at each age and reflecting back on where I found myself at each – a perspective I've cultivated in *One/Two* – is that the rich interiority of childhood carries one well beyond the brief moment of youth. The experiences of the young self in the worlds we come from and outgrow, can nourish us still. When I look at this book completed, I see *One/Two* as a collection of votive images, and its prose poems as a chronicling of self-making; the making of the self from the intuitions of girlhood carried into the present, and the making of sense as a collection of aesthetic experiences.[23] The sense I'm driven to make is varied, but it's themes connected: How are one's aesthetic inclinations formed over time? How does one unfold as a political being? How do the sometimes invisible ways we care for each other, or create knowledge, invest in our own making of freedom? What experimentations, rehearsed in community, help us expand the possibilities we believe exist for ourselves? These rehearsals toward autonomy, or dignity, or sense-making - what we might call practices of freedom – might be enacted in any of the spaces we find ourselves in, material or abstract: in our neighborhoods, in our ancestry, in friendships, through decadence, outside the law, in nurturing our children, in coping mechanisms, in experiencing grief, or in our imaginations. It is this question of how we fashion our own utopias out of situations of dispossession, or how the marginalized become cultural producers, that grounds my creative practice and my interests as a maker. Art and art forms born of exclusion are one of the great American stories, after all, and one I hold as an inheritance.

[1] Sarah Manguso, *300 Arguments*, (Minneapolis: Graywolf Press, 2017).

[2] Maggie Nelson, *Like Love: Essay and Conversations*, (Minneapolis: Graywolf Press, 2024).

[3] Maggie Nelson, *Like Love: Essay and Conversations*, 169.

[4] Moyra Davey, *Long Life, Cool White: Photographs and Essays*, (Cambridge, MA: Harvard Art Museums; CT: Yale University Press, 2008), 96.

[5] Maggie Nelson, *The Argonauts*, (Minneapolis: Graywolf Press, 2015), 43.

[6] Brand, *A Map to the Door of No Return*, (New York: Picador, 2024), 27.

[7] George Kouvaros, *The Old Greeks: Photography, Cinema, Migration*, (Perth, Western Australia: UWA Publishing, 2018), 26.

[8] Maggie Nelson, *On Freedom: Four Songs of Care and Constraint*, (Minneapolis: Graywolf Press, 2021), 208.

[9] Saidiya Hartman, "Afterword: A Room with History," in Dionne Brand, *A Map to the Door of No Return*, 227-236.

[10] Kouvaros, 173.

[11] Saidiya Hartman, *Lose Your Mother: A Journey Along the Atlantic Slave Route*, (New York: Farrar, Straus, Giroux, 2007), 103.

[12] Kouvaros, 169.

[13] Fred Moten, *The Little Edges*, (Middletown, CT: Wesleyan University Press, 2015), 32-33.

[14] Kouvaros, 19-20.

[15] Dionne Brand, *The Blue Clerk*, (Durham: Duke University Press, 2018), 34-36.

[16] Brand, *A Map to the Door of No Return*, 93.

[17] Brand, *A Map to the Door of No Return*, 108-109.

[18] The Invisible Committee, *To Our Friends*, trans. Robert Hurley (Los Angeles: Semiotext(e), 2015)

[19] Billy-Ray Belcourt, *History of My Brief Body*, (Minneapolis: Graywolf Press, 2020), 50.

[20] Nelson, *Like Love*, 32.

[21] Stefano Harney and Fred Moten, *The Undercommons: Fugitive Planning & Black Study*, (New York: Minor Compositions, 2013).

[22] Robin D.G. Kelley, ˆFreedom Dreams: The Black Radical Imagination, (Boston: Beacon Press, 2022).

[23] Dionne Brand, *A Map to the Door of No Return*, 197.

ACKNOWLEDGMENTS

The impulse to take my personal mythology as the content of art making, and the belief that what is true for me could be useful to others, was not won on my own. I owe a great debt to the work of Khiara Bridges, Tommie Shelby, Robin D.G. Kelley, Ta-Nehisi Coates, Sheryl Cashin, Matthew Desmond, Kathryn Edin, Virginia Eubanks, and Christina Sharpe for the ways in which they give intellectual rigor to my intuitions.

A core sense of lineage for me is with the artists and thinkers with whom I feel connection. The intellectual company I kept while secluded in the studio working on this book was with Saidiya Hartman, Stefano Harney, Jack Halberstam, Fred Moten, and Maggie Nelson. Their light is in my work, and I hope it goes out into the world in their continuum.

I'm grateful to have found the scholarship of George Kouvaros. His work on the resonance of photography and cinema in understanding the particularity of the 1.5-generation immigrant's experience has been invaluable. He centers the role of images for those who emigrated from their country of origin in childhood, and are then compelled to reconstitute a history from aesthetic and narrative fragments.

In writing about migration, loss, nostos, origins, and longing, especially in an urban context, I was nourished by the work of Dionne Brand. Hers is a sensibility that I feel at home with. Reading her filled me with something akin to courage so that I could take seriously the words coming up in my own mind in the three tremendous months when I was blessed with the appearance of verses, when I thought I was making a photobook. I live in gratitude for these manifestations of grace in my vocation.

A constant companion in the making of the book is my collaborator Sierra Lawhead. We share a natural understanding of each other's aesthetics, making working together flow with ease and clarity. My actualization as a book maker is linked with her generosity and talent.

The Athens Social Atlas project has been an indispensable resource in learning about the social geography of the city. In particular, I've relied on the research of Myofa Nikolina of Harokopio University to inform my understanding of refugee and social housing in Athens. I wouldn't have known how to decipher what I was seeing in the Athenian landscape without it.

I'm grateful to the following poets for their support: Vanessa Aricco, Aaron Graham, and José Olivarez, for reading the poems with a sensitive engagement, but mostly for snapping in delight and encouragement during an anonymous review of poetry manuscripts hosted by the Ohio Arts Council; Ajanaé Dawkins for being a first reader, and for the nudge to make something out of the imagery of the popcorn ceiling that I casually shared with her.

I want to recognize the impact of the Ohio Arts Council on my life as an artist. The OAC has recognized my work through the Individual Excellence Award, and has supported the making of this work with an Artist Opportunities Grant. The Greater Columbus Arts Council has also championed my art practice every step of the way through artist grants that support the making of new work. I'm thankful that the GCAC has invested in me as an artist, and in the making of this project.

I wish to thank the women whose talents and generosity have nourished my art practice: Julia Cameron, guide and art mother, Elizabeth Clemants, whose gifts have, without exaggeration, changed the course of my life and made me available to myself, and Janice Glowski, whose first gesture of belief in my work marks every subsequent unfolding of it.

Many thanks to my Columbus she-pack, Sara Bartley, Kate Curlis and Aline Yamada. Watching them work with the stuff of life and of motherhood, and doing the same by their sides, has been as formative as any experience of youth. I'm inspired by their fearlessness and their insights.

I'm thankful to my cousin Efi Hakiami, who connects me with a past I haven't known myself, and whose kindness is an inspiration to anyone lucky enough to find themselves in her midst. Many of the photographs I was able to make in Athens were thanks to her joyously making cookies with the children while I explored the parts of Athens that held secrets I needed to uncover.

I want to thank my mother, Elli, for her courage, work ethic and constant devotion. Her generosity is unlike anyone's I have ever come across. It astounds me, and bridges the other distances in our relationship. When I look around the home I've made with my own family, she is everywhere: in the artistry of textiles, in the embroideries and the women's work, in the kitchen, and in the house itself. I also extend my appreciation to my brother, Yiorgos Sarrinikolaou, for modelling excellence and political integrity, and for our shared sense of the wholesome and the life-affirming. I have known and been known by him.

My closest friends Glen Parker, Jack Roche, and Maryana Zubok light up my life like nothing else. The adult version of our friendships are one of my greatest blessings. The tenor of what we share is so rarefied, vulnerable, and precious that it feels outside of the confines of everyday life. There is no fuller way to honor this than to have made something of our love and experiences in these pages.

The deepest gratitude goes to my husband Efthimi. I'm awed every day by what we've made together, and by what we've given one another. This book is a testament to our adventures, and to our capacity of seeing through shared eyes.

I thank my children, Anaïs and Savva, for loving so freely, for their radiance, and for the pleasure of sharing our lives. What a joy it is to hold their care at my center! I hope this work is inspiring to them when the time comes to reflect on their own childhoods.

MAGDA PARASIDIS is a visual artist and designer born in Athens, Greece. She immigrated to New York City in 1980, settling in a public housing project in Queens. Parasidis's text-based art and photography has been exhibited widely, and is held in both private and public collections. The monograph Magda Parasidis: *Ghosts in Sunlight* was published in 2021 to accompany a solo exhibition at Otterbein University in Columbus, Ohio, where she teaches the history of art in protest movements. Her debut photobook and poetry collection, *One/Two*, is the inaugural title from Holy Harlot Press.

magdaparasidis.com
@magdaparasidis

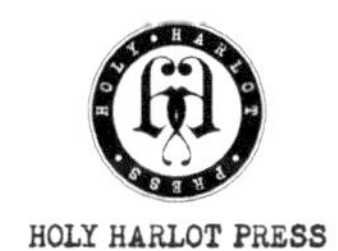

HOLY HARLOT PRESS

www.ingramcontent.com/pod-product-compliance
Lightning Source LLC
LaVergne TN
LVHW072029110826
845147LV00001BA/11
9798992564600